Important Instruction

Use the URL or QR code provided below to unlock all the online learning resources included with this Grade 4 to 5 summer learning activities workbook.

URL	QR Code
Visit the URL below for online registration **http://www.lumoslearning.com/a/tg4-5**	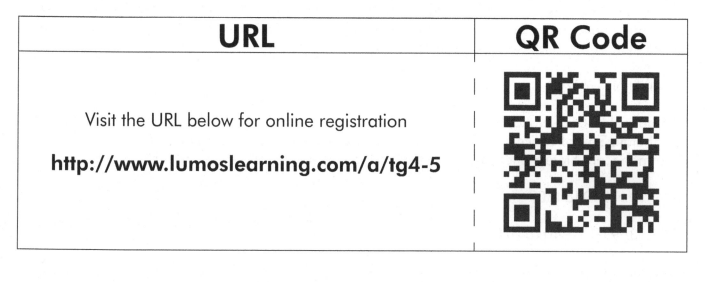

Your online access includes;

- Skills practice resources for Grade 5 Math and ELA
- Grade-appropriate passages to improve reading skills
- Grade 4 vocabulary quizzes
- Access to Lumos Flashcube - An interactive tool to improve vocabulary
- Educational videos, worksheets, standards information and more

Additional Benefits of Online Registration

- Entry to Lumos Weekly Summer Photo Contest
- Entry to Lumos Short Story Competition

Lumos Learning
Developed by Expert Teachers

Summer Learning HeadStart, Grade 4 to 5: Fun Activities Plus Math, Reading, and Language Workbooks

Contributing Author	-	Jessica Fisher
Contributing Author	-	Mary Evans Rumley
Contributing Author	-	Julie C. Lyons
Contributing Editor	-	George Smith
Contributing Author	-	Marisa Adams
Executive Producer	-	Mukunda Krishnaswamy
Designer and Illustrator	-	Sowmya R.

First Edition - 2020

ISBN 10: 1940484707

ISBN 13: 978-1-940484-70-9

Printed in the United States of America

Last updated - April 2022

For permissions and additional information contact us

Lumos Information Services, LLC
PO Box 1575, Piscataway, NJ 08855-1575
http://www.LumosLearning.com

Email: support@lumoslearning.com
Tel: (732) 384-0146
Fax: (866) 283-6471

Lumos Learning
Developed by Expert Teachers

Table of Contents

Introduction			1
	How to Use This Workbook Effectively During Summer		6

Summer Practice and Fun Activities

Week 1 — Summer Practice P 9 - 30

Day 1	Number Sentence	9
	Finding Details in the Story	10
	Daily Challenge ⊕	
Day 2	Real World Problems	12
	Inferring	13
	Daily Challenge ⊕	
Day 3	Multi-Step Problems	15
	Finding the Theme	16
	Daily Challenge ⊕	
Day 4	Number Theory	18
	Summarizing the Text	19
	Daily Challenge ⊕	
Day 5	Patterns	21
	Describing Characters	22
	Daily Challenge ⊕	
Learn Sign Language		26

⊕ Online Activity | Reading Assignment | Vocabulary Practice | Summer Diary

Week 2 — Summer Practice P 31 - 51

Day 1	Place Value	31
	Describing the Setting	32
	Daily Challenge ⊕	
Day 2	Compare Numbers and Expanded Notation	35
	Describing Events	36
	Daily Challenge ⊕	
Day 3	Rounding Numbers	39
	Figurative Language	40
	Daily Challenge ⊕	
Day 4	Addition & Subtraction	42
	Text Structure	43
	Daily Challenge ⊕	
Day 5	Multiplication	46
	Point of View	47
	Daily Challenge ⊕	
7 Tips to Improve Your Baseball Skills		49

⊕ Online Activity | Reading Assignment | Vocabulary Practice | Summer Diary

Week 3

Summer Practice

P 52 - 73

Day 1	Division	52	
	Visual Connections	53	
	Daily Challenge 🌐		
Day 2	Equivalent Fractions	56	
	Comparing and Contrasting	57	
	Daily Challenge 🌐		
Day 3	Compare Fractions	60	
	It's All in the Details	61	
	Daily Challenge 🌐		
Day 4	Adding and Subtracting Fractions	64	
	The Main Idea	65	
	Daily Challenge 🌐		
Day 5	Adding and Subtracting Fractions through Decompositions	68	
	Using Details to Explain the Text	69	
	Daily Challenge 🌐		

Draw and Color 71

🌐 Online Activity	Reading Assignment	Vocabulary Practice	Summer Diary

Week 4

Summer Practice

P 74 - 91

Day 1	Adding and Subtracting Mixed Numbers	74	
	What Does it Mean?	75	
	Daily Challenge 🌐		
Day 2	Adding and Subtracting Fractions in Word Problems	77	
	How is it Written?	78	
	Daily Challenge 🌐		
Day 3	Multiplying Fractions	80	
	Comparing Different Versions of the Same Event	81	
	Daily Challenge 🌐		
Day 4	Multiplying Fractions by a Whole Number	83	
	Using Text Features to Gather Information	84	
	Daily Challenge 🌐		
Day 5	Multiplying Fractions in Word Problems	86	
	Finding the Evidence	87	
	Daily Challenge 🌐		

Rock Out! Tips for Beginning Rock Climbers 89

🌐 Online Activity	Reading Assignment	Vocabulary Practice	Summer Diary

Week 5 — Summer Practice — P 92 - 105

Day 1	10 to 100 Equivalent Fractions	92
	Integrating Information	93
	Daily Challenge 🌐	
Day 2	Convert Fractions to Decimals	96
	Pronouns	97
	Daily Challenge 🌐	
Day 3	Compare Decimals	98
	Progressive Verb Tense	99
	Daily Challenge 🌐	
Day 4	Units of Measurement	100
	Modal Auxiliary Verbs	101
	Daily Challenge 🌐	
Day 5	Measurement Problems	102
	Adjectives and Adverbs	103
	Daily Challenge 🌐	
Maze Game		104

🌐 Online Activity | Reading Assignment | Vocabulary Practice | Summer Diary

Week 6 — Summer Practice — P 106 - 121

Day 1	Perimeter & Area	106
	Prepositional Phrases	107
	Daily Challenge 🌐	
Day 2	Representing and Interpreting Data	108
	Complete Sentences	110
	Daily Challenge 🌐	
Day 3	Angle Measurement	112
	Frequently Confused Words	113
	Daily Challenge 🌐	
Day 4	Measuring Turned Angles	115
	How is it Capitalized?	116
	Daily Challenge 🌐	
Day 5	Measuring and Sketching Angles	118
	What's the Punctuation?	119
	Daily Challenge 🌐	

🌐 Online Activity | Reading Assignment | Vocabulary Practice | Summer Diary

Week 7 — Summer Practice — P 122 - 136

Day		Page
Day 1	Adding and Subtracting Angle Measurements	122
	How is it Spelled?	123
	Daily Challenge ⊕	
Day 2	Points, Lines, Rays, and Segments	125
	Word Choice: Attending to Precision	126
	Daily Challenge ⊕	
Day 3	Angles	127
	Punctuating for Effect!	128
	Daily Challenge ⊕	
Day 4	Classifying Plane (2-D) Shapes	129
	Finding the Meaning	130
	Daily Challenge ⊕	
Day 5	Symmetry	131
	Context Clues	132
	Daily Challenge ⊕	
	Cross Word Puzzles	134

⊕ Online Activity | Reading Assignment | Vocabulary Practice | Summer Diary

Week 8 — Summer Practice — P 137 - 149

Day		Page
Day 1	Number Sentences	137
	The Meaning of Words	138
	Daily Challenge ⊕	
Day 2	Real World Problems	139
	For Your Reference	140
	Daily Challenge ⊕	
Day 3	Multi-Step Problems	142
	Similes and Metaphors	143
	Daily Challenge ⊕	
Day 4	Number Theory	145
	Idiomatic Expressions and Proverbs	146
	Daily Challenge ⊕	
Day 5	Patterns	147
	Synonyms and Antonyms	148
	Daily Challenge ⊕	

⊕ Online Activity | Reading Assignment | Vocabulary Practice | Summer Diary

Week 9 **Summer Practice** P 150 - 161	Day 1	Place Value	150
		Academic and Domain Specific 4th Grade Words	151
		Daily Challenge 🌐	
	Day 2	Compare Numbers and Expanded Notation	152
		Conjunctions and Interjections	153
		Daily Challenge 🌐	
	Day 3	Rounding Numbers	154
		What's the Verb?	155
		Daily Challenge 🌐	
	Day 4	Addition & Subtraction	156
		Same Word Different Meanings	157
		Daily Challenge 🌐	
	Day 5	Multiplication	158
		Point of View	159
		Daily Challenge 🌐	

🌐 Online Activity | Reading Assignment | Vocabulary Practice | Summer Diary

Week 10	Lumos Short Story Competition 2022	
	Details of Lumos Short Story Competition 2022	162
	Winning Stories from 2021 & 2020	164

Answer Key and Detailed Explanation	**166**

Blogs

- Stop! In The Name Of Education: Prevent Summer Learning Loss With 7 Simple Steps · · · 217
- Summer Reading: Questions To Ask That Promote Comprehension · · · 219
- Beating The Brain Drain Through Literacy: Webinar Recap With Printable Activity Sheet · · · 221
- Summer Is Here! Keep Your Child's Writing Skills Sharp With Online Games · · · 224
- Webinar "cliff Notes" For Beating Summer Academic Loss: An Informative Guide To Parents · · · 226
- Valuable Learning Experiences: A Summer Activity Guide For Parents · · · 229

Additional Information	**231**

Introduction

What is Summer Academic Learning Loss?

What is Summer Academic Learning Loss? Studies show that if students take a standardized test at the end of the school year, and then repeat that test when they return in the fall, they will lose approximately four to six weeks of learning. In other words, they could potentially miss more questions in the fall than they would in the spring. This loss is commonly referred to as the summer slide.

When these standardized testing scores drop an average of one month, it causes teachers to spend at least the first four to five weeks, on average, re-teaching critical material. In terms of math, students typically lose an average of two and a half months of skills, and when reading and math losses are combined, it averages three months; it may even be lower for students in lower-income homes.

And on average, the three areas students will typically lose ground in are spelling, vocabulary, and mathematics.

How can You Help Combat Summer Learning Loss?

Like anything, academics are something that requires practice, and if they are not used regularly, you run the risk of losing them. Because of this, it is imperative your children work to keep their minds sharp over the summer. There are many ways to keep your children engaged over the summer, and we're going to explore some of the most beneficial.

Start with School:

Your best source of information is your child's school. Have a conversation with your child's teacher. Tell them you are interested in working on some academics over the summer and ask what suggestions they might have. Be sure to ask about any areas your child may be struggling in and for a list of books to read over the summer. Also, talk to your child's counselor. They may have recommendations of local summer activities that will relate back to the schools and what your child needs to know. Finally, ask the front office staff for any information on currently existing after school programs (the counselor may also be able to provide this). Although after school programs may end shortly, the organizations running them will often have information on summer camps. Many of these are often free or at a very low cost to you and your family.

Stay Local:

Scour your local area for free or low-cost activities and events. Most museums will have dollar days of some kind where you can get money-off admission for going on a certain day of the week or a certain time. Zoos will often do the same thing. Take lunch to the park and eat outside, talking about the leaves, flowers, or anything else you can find there. Your child can pick one favorite thing and research it. Attend concerts or shows put on by local artists, musicians, or other vendors. There are many other options available; you just have to explore and find them. The key here is to engage your children. Have them look online with you or search the local newspapers/magazines. Allow them to plan the itinerary, or work with you on it, and when they get back, have them write a journal about the activity. Or, even better, have them write a letter or email to a family member about what they did.

Practice Daily:

Whether the choice is a family activity or experiencing the local environment, staying academically focused is the key is to keep your child engaged every day. This daily practice helps keep student's minds sharp and focused, ensuring they will be able to not only retain the knowledge they have learned, but in many cases begin to move ahead for the next year.

Summer Strategies for Students

Summer is here, which brings a time of excitement, relaxation, and fun. School is the last thing on your mind, but that doesn't mean learning has to be on vacation too. In fact, learning is as just as important and be just as fun (if not more) during the summer months than during the school year.

Did you know that during the summer:

- Students often lose an average of 2 and ½ months of math skills
- Students often lose 2 months of reading skills
- Teachers spend at least the first 4 to 5 weeks of the next school year reteaching important skills and concepts

Your brain is like a muscle, and like any muscle, it must be worked out regularly, and like this, your language arts and math skills are something that requires practice; if you do not use them regularly, you run the risk of losing them. So, it is very important you keep working through the summer. But, it doesn't always have to be 'school' type of work. There are many ways to stay engaged, and we're going to spend a little time looking through them.

Read and Write as Often as Possible

Reading is one of the most important things you can do to keep your brain sharp and engaged. Here are some tips to remember about summer reading:

- Often, summer is the perfect time to find and read new books or books you have always been curious about. However, without your teacher, you may struggle with finding a book that is appropriate for your reading level. In this case, you just have to remember the five-finger rule: open a book to a random page and begin reading aloud, holding up one finger for each word you cannot say or do not know. If you have more than five fingers visible, then the book is probably too hard to read.

- Reading goes beyond books; there are so many other ways to read. Magazines are a great way to keep kids connected to learning, and they encourage so many different activities. National Geographic Kids, Ranger Rick, and American Girl are just a few examples. As silly as it may sound, you can also read the backs of cereal boxes and billboards to work on reading confidence and fluency, and learn many new things along the way! And thinking completely outside the box, you can also read when singing karaoke. Reading the words as they flash across the screen is a great way to build fluency. You can also turn the closed captioning on when a TV show is on to encourage literacy and reading fluency.

But writing is equally as important, and there are many things you can do to write over the summer:

- First, consider keeping a journal of your summer activities. You can detail the things you do, places you go, even people you meet. Be sure to include as much description as possible – sights, sounds, colors should all be included so you can easily remember and visualize the images. But the wonderful thing about a journal is that spelling and sentence structure are not as important. It's just the practice of actually writing;   that is where your focus should be. The other nice thing about a journal is that this informal writing is just for you; with journal writing you don't have to worry about anything, you just have to start writing.

- But if you want a little more depth to your journaling, and you want to share it with others, there is a fantastic opportunity for you with blogging. With parental approval, you can create a blog online where you can share your summer experiences with friends, family, or any others. The wonderful thing about blogs is that you can play with the privacy settings and choose whom you want to see your blogs. You can make it private, where only the individuals who you send the link to can see it, or you can choose for it to be public where anyone can read it. Of course, if you are keeping a blog, you will have to make it a little more formal and pay attention to spelling, grammar, and sentences simply because you want to make sure your blog is pleasing to those who are reading it. Some popular places to post blogs are Blogger, Wordpress, Squarespace, and Quillpad.

Practice Math in Real Life

One way you can keep your brain sharp is by looking at the world around you and finding ways to include math. In this case, we're thinking of fun, practical ways to practice in your daily life.

- First, have some fun this summer with being in charge of some family projects. Suggest a fun project to complete with a parent or grandparent; decide on an area to plant some new bushes or maybe a small home project you can work on together. You can help design the project and maybe even research the best plants to plant or the best way to build the project. Then write the shopping list, making sure you determine the correct amount of supplies you will need. Without even realizing it, you would have used some basic math calculations and geometry to complete the project.

- You can also find math in shopping for groceries or while doing some back to school shopping. For each item that goes into the cart, estimate how much it will be and keep a running estimation of the total cost. Make it a competition before you go by estimating what your total bill will be and see who comes the closest. Or, you can even try and compete to see who can determine the correct total amount of tax that will be needed. And a final mental game to play while shopping is to determine the change you should receive when paying with cash. Not only is this a good skill to practice math, more importantly, helps you make sure you're getting the correct change.

- You can even use everyday math if you are doing any traveling this summer, and there are many fun ways to do this. Traveling requires money, and someone has to be in charge of the budget. You can volunteer to be the family accountant. Make a budget for the trip and keep all the receipts. Tally up the cost of the trip and even try to break it up by category – food, fun, hotels, gas are just a few of the categories you can include. For those of you who might be looking for even more of a challenge, you can calculate what percentage of your budget has been spent on each category as well.

- And traveling by car gives many opportunities as well. Use the car odometer to calculate how far you have traveled. For an added challenge, you can see if you can calculate how much gas you used as well as how many gallons of gas per mile have been used.

Practice Daily:

Whether the choice is a family activity or experiencing the local environment, staying academically focused is the key to keep your mind engaged every day. That daily practice keeps your brain sharp and focused, and helps to ensure that you are not only able to retain the knowledge you learned last year but also to get a jump start on next year's success too!

How to Use This Workbook Effectively During Summer

This book offers a variety of state standards aligned resources, in both printed and online format, to help students learn during Summer months.

The activities in the book are organized by week and aligned with the 4th grade learning standards. We encourage you to start at the beginning of Summer holidays. During each week, students can complete daily Math and English practice. There are five daily practice worksheets for each week. Students can log in to the online program once a week to complete reading, vocabulary and writing practice. Students can work on fun activity anytime during that week. Additionally, students can record their Summer activity through the online program.

Please note that the online program also includes access to 5th grade learning resources. This section of the online program could be used to help students to get a glimpse of what they would be learning in the next grade level.

Weekly Fun Summer Photo Contest

Take a picture of your summer fun activity and share it on Twitter or Instagram

Use the **#SummerLearning** mention

@LumosLearning on Twitter or

@lumos.learning on Instagram

Tag friends and increase your chances of winning the contest

Participate and stand a chance to WIN $50 Amazon gift card!

Take Advantage of the Online Resources

To access the online resources included with this book, parents and teachers can register with a FREE account. With each free signup, student accounts can be associated to enable online access for them.

Once the registration is complete, the login credentials for the created accounts will be sent in email to the id used during signup. Students can log in to their student accounts to get started with their summer learning. Parents can use the parent portal to keep track of student's progress.

URL	QR Code
Visit the URL below for online registration **http://www.lumoslearning.com/a/tg4-5**	

Lumos Short Story Competition 2022

**Write a Short Story
Based On Your Summer Experiences**

Get A Chance To Win $100 Cash Prize

+

1 Year Free Subscription To Lumos StepUp

+

Trophy With Certificate

How can my child participate in this competition?

Step 1
Visit **www.lumoslearning.com/a/tg4-5** to register for online fun summer program.

Step 2
After registration, your child can upload their summer story by logging into the student portal and clicking on Lumos Short Story Competition 2022.
Last date for submission is August 31, 2022

How is this competition judged?
Lumos teachers will review students submissions in Sep 2022. Quality of submission would be judged based on creativity, coherence and writing skills.

We recommend short stories that are less than 500 words.

1. Andrew is twice as old as his brother, Josh. Which equation could be used to figure out Andrew's age if Josh's age, n, is unknown?

   (A) a = n + 2
   (B) a = n ÷ 2
   (C) n = a + 2
   (D) a = 2 x n

2. Mandy bought 28 marbles. She wants to give the same number of marbles to each of her four friends. What equation or number sentence would she use to find the number of marbles each friend will get?

   (A) 28 - 4 = n
   (B) 28 ÷ 4 = n
   (C) 28 + 4 = n
   (D) 28 - 4 = n

3. What number does n represent?
   3 + 6 + n = 22

   (A) n = 9
   (B) n = 13
   (C) n = 18
   (D) n = 31

4. Write an equation to show how many crayons are below.

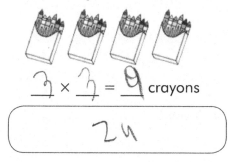

   _3_ × _3_ = _9_ crayons

   24

"The Elephant Who Saw the World . . .," Mary started speaking. It was Friday, and the students had to share their creative writing stories of the week.

Mary loved writing, and this was her favorite part of the week, when they were able to make up stories for creative writing. She enjoyed it so much that she became really good at it. Even at home on the weekends when she didn't have much homework, she would sit in her room for hours and create stories to share with her friends and family. Her parents always supported her and were her biggest fans.

However, there was one part about every Friday at school that Mary did not enjoy, and that was when she had to share her story in front of the class. The teacher made all of the children share on Friday afternoons, and this made Mary very nervous. She was shy, and although she knew her teacher was right, she didn't like it.

Sitting and listening to the other children, Mary heard her name called. It was her turn to share. She got out of her seat slowly, walked to the front of the room and began.

5. What is the title of Mary's story?

Ⓐ The Elephant Who Liked Candy
Ⓑ The Elephant Who Saw the World
Ⓒ The Elephant Who Wanted to See the World
Ⓓ The Girl who Hated Writing

6. What didn't Mary like doing?

Ⓐ Writing stories
Ⓑ Having her stories corrected by the teacher
Ⓒ Reading her stories in front of the class
Ⓓ Going to school

7. Why was Mary reading her story in front of the class?

Ⓐ It was something she loved to do.
Ⓑ Her classmates asked her to.
Ⓒ Every Friday the children had to share their creative writing stories.
Ⓓ Her parents wanted her to.

Disneyworld- Here We Come! Part - II

Before we knew it, it was daylight again. Mom was hustling us out of bed and into the kitchen for breakfast. She said to eat hearty as we had many more miles to go before we reached our final destination. So thankful that my grandmother cooked her best oatmeal for us topped with cinnamon, brown sugar, strawberries, and whipped cream! Who could ask for anything more? Yummy!!

Then it was load back into the car and get on the road. This time Mom found an oldies radio station and she was singing along with Patsy Cline, Tennessee Ernie Ford, and Frank Sinatra. Talk about strange music that none of us knew except her! Valerie and I played a game of travel trivia which was sort of fun and of course, Daniel, was back on his video games!

For lunch we stopped at a roadside park and had the sandwiches our grandmother had packed for us along with an apple and sweet iced tea. When we got back on the road, not a sound could be heard. I figured out later that all of us kids had fallen asleep.

A loud bang awoke us as Mom clapped her hands and proclaimed our arrival to the Holiday Inn at Disneyworld! I could not tell you who was the most excited as we were all yelling sounds of glee and running around the car to get our luggage out. Mom registered us for our room and we were giggling uncontrollably.

8. How did the author's mom wake the kids once she arrived at the hotel? Write your answer in the box below.

> she was clapped her hands

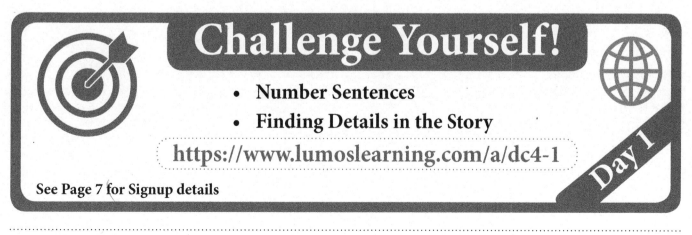

Day 2

1. There are four boxes of pears. Each box has 24 pears. How many pears are there total?

    Ⓐ 72 pears
    Ⓑ 48 pears
    Ⓒ 96 pears
    Ⓓ 88 pears

2. Trevor has a collection of 450 baseball cards. He wants to place them into an album. He can fit 15 baseball cards on each page. How can Trevor figure out how many pages he will need to fit in all of his cards?

    Ⓐ By adding 450 and 15
    Ⓑ By subtracting 15 from 450
    Ⓒ By multiplying 450 by 15
    Ⓓ By dividing 450 by 15

3. Bow Wow Pet Shop has 12 dogs. Each dog had 4 puppies. How many puppies does the shop have in all?

    Ⓐ 16 puppies
    Ⓑ 12 puppies
    Ⓒ 48 puppies
    Ⓓ 36 puppies

4. Charlie has $938. He wants to buy gifts for his 15 family members. He wants to spend the same amount of money (in dollars) for each person. With the remaining money, he buys a pen worth $3. How much money will he have left over after his purchases? Write your answer in the box below.

    $ 5

I found a shell, a curly one;
Lying on the sand.
I picked it up and took it home,
Held tightly in my hand.
Mommy looked at it and then,
She held it to my ear,
And from the shell there came a song
Soft and sweet and clear.
I was surprised, I listened hard,
And it was really true:
If you can find a nice big shell,
You'll hear the singing too.
--Unknown

5. Why was the poet surprised?

Ⓐ She found a curly shell on the beach.
Ⓑ Her mother put it to her ear.
Ⓒ She didn't expect to hear a song from the shell.
Ⓓ She was frightened of the shell.

Alexander the Great

Nearly two thousand five hundred years ago, there lived a king called Alexander the Great. He was the son of Philip II of Macedonia. When prince Alexander was a boy, a magnificent horse that was for sale was brought to the court of his father. The animal was to be sold for thirteen talents. Talents are ancient coins. Many were eager to buy the horse, but no one could get close enough to saddle the restless animal. He was wild and impossible to ride.

Alexander pleaded with his father to let him try. Realizing that the horse was terrified of its own shadow, he turned the horse towards the sun so that its shadow fell behind it. This calmed the horse, and the prince proudly rode away. Observing this, his father said, "My son, look for a kingdom worthy of your greatness. Macedonia is too small for you."

That is exactly what Alexander tried to do when he grew up. He fought many battles and always rode Bucephalus (that was the horse's name.) Friendship and trust grew between the man and his horse. When Bucephalus died of wounds received in battle, Alexander was heartbroken and deeply mourned the loss of his horse.

6. According to the passage, why do you think the horse was unrideable and wild?

Ⓐ because it was angry
Ⓑ because it was hungry
Ⓒ because it was scared
Ⓓ because it was good at riding

Cindy's mom called her to supper. When Cindy arrived in the kitchen, she looked at the food on the stove and made a face. She looked in the freezer and saw a frozen pizza and asked her mom if she could cook it instead.

7. What can you infer from Cindy's actions?

Ⓐ That she was excited about what her mother had cooked
Ⓑ She was not very hungry for dinner.
Ⓒ She didn't think the meal was ready.
Ⓓ She didn't like what her mother cooked for dinner.

The Wolf and the Lamb

A Wolf, meeting with a Lamb astray from the fold, resolved not to lay violent hands on him, but to find some plea, which should justify to the Lamb himself his right to eat him. He then addressed him: "Sirrah, last year you grossly insulted me." "Indeed," bleated the Lamb in a mournful tone of voice, "I was not then born." Then said the Wolf: "You feed in my pasture." "No, good sir," replied the Lamb, "I have not yet tasted grass." Again said the Wolf: "You drink from my well." "No," exclaimed the Lamb, "I never yet drank water, for as yet my mother's milk is both food and drink to me." On which the Wolf seized him, and ate him up, saying: "Well! I won't remain supperless, even though you refute every one of my imputations."The tyrant will always find a pretext for his tyranny, and it is useless for the innocent to try by reasoning to get justice, when the oppressor intends to be unjust.

8. What was the wolf trying to do when he wanted to eat the lamb? Circle the correct answer choice.

Ⓐ Justify his pleasure.
Ⓑ Prove he was stronger.
Ⓒ Not eat the lamb.
Ⓓ All of the above.

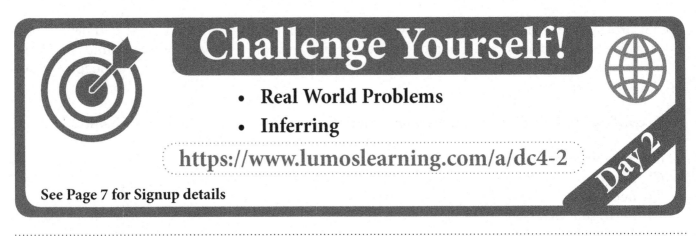

Challenge Yourself!

- **Real World Problems**
- **Inferring**

https://www.lumoslearning.com/a/dc4-2

See Page 7 for Signup details

Day 2

Day 3

1. Kristian purchased four textbooks which cost $34.99 each, and a backpack that cost $19.98. Estimate the total cost of the items he purchased. (You do not need to consider tax.)

   Ⓐ $90.00
   Ⓑ $160.00
   Ⓒ $120.00
   Ⓓ $55.00

2. During the last three games of the season, the attendance at the Tigers' home games was 14,667; 16,992; and 18,124. Estimate the total attendance for these three games. Round to the nearest thousand.

   Ⓐ 60,000
   Ⓑ 45,000
   Ⓒ 50,000
   Ⓓ 47,000

3. Steven keeps his baseball cards in an album. He has filled 147 pages of the album. He can fit 9 cards on each page. Which of the following statements is true?

   Ⓐ Steven has more than 2,000 baseball cards.
   Ⓑ Steven has between 1,000 and 1,500 baseball cards.
   Ⓒ Steven has between 1,500 and 2,000 baseball cards.
   Ⓓ Steven has less than 1,000 baseball cards.

4. Charlie sells paintings. He charges 35 dollars for a large painting and m dollars for a small painting. He sold 8 large paintings and 6 small paintings and earned $412. How much did he charge for each small painting? Write your answer in the box below.

Fred Goes to the Dentist

Fred had never been to the dentist. All of his life he had heard horror stories about the buzzing drills, the huge needles, and the scary tools that the dentist used to torture his patients. Since none of his teeth were hurting, Fred just couldn't understand why his mom was insisting on taking him to the dentist. She told him that it was important to visit the dentist each year to have his teeth checked and cleaned. This seemed silly to Fred because he cleaned his teeth everyday by brushing and flossing them, but nothing would change his mother's mind. He found it hard to believe that she would think it was a good idea to take him somewhere to be tortured. However, he had no choice but to go.

On the way to the dentist, Fred's imagination went wild. He pictured walking into a room with a huge chair that the dentist would strap him to. He could just see the dentist pulling out a huge drill and drilling his tooth while his mother and several others held him in the chair. By the time he got to the dentist's office, he was shaking all over.

Surprisingly, the office was nothing like he expected. The dentist was friendly, and the chair was comfortable. It didn't have any straps. He looked around the room and didn't see any huge drills or torture devices. He was relieved when all the dentist did was look in his mouth, show him how to properly brush and floss his teeth, and give him a balloon. His mom made another appointment to have his teeth cleaned in six months. Maybe this wouldn't be as bad as he had thought it would be.

5. What is the theme of the passage?

Ⓐ Dentists are good people so don't worry about seeing them.
Ⓑ Moms usually know best so trust them.
Ⓒ Things are usually not as bad as you think they will be.
Ⓓ An imagination is good but it can make things seem scary sometimes.

Opal walked into the store not wanting to do what she had planned. She knew when she took the makeup without paying for it that it was wrong. She felt so guilty. She knew she couldn't keep the makeup. So, gathering up all of her courage, she walked over to the security officer and confessed what she had done. He admonished her for shoplifting but let her off with a warning because she had been honest. She felt very relieved.

6. What is the theme of the above passage?

Ⓐ The unknown can be scary.
Ⓑ It is best to be honest.
Ⓒ Don't cry over spilled milk.
Ⓓ Mom knows best.

Libby's grandmother didn't have much money, so she couldn't buy Libby an expensive present for Christmas like her other grandmother could. She didn't want to buy her a cheap toy that wouldn't last long, but she just couldn't afford the things that were on Libby's wish list. She decided to make Libby a quilt. She was concerned that her granddaughter wouldn't like the gift, but it was the best that she could do.

When Christmas day arrived, Grandmother went to Libby's house. She saw all of the nice gifts that her granddaughter had received. She was worried as Libby began to open her present. Libby squealed with delight when she saw the handmade quilt. She ran and hugged her grandmother and thanked her. She ran and put the new quilt on her bed. The rest of the day she talked about how much she loved the quilt, especially since her grandmother had made it all by hand.

7. What is the theme of the above passage?

Ⓐ It is not the cost of the gift that matters but the thought and love put into it.
Ⓑ Expensive gifts are better than homemade ones.
Ⓒ Homemade gifts are as good as expensive toys.
Ⓓ Good manners have positive results.

I found a shell, a curly one;
Lying on the sand.
I picked it up and took it home,
Held tightly in my hand.
Mommy looked at it and then,
She held it to my ear,
And from the shell there came a song
Soft and sweet and clear.
I was surprised, I listened hard,
And it was really true:
If you can find a nice big shell,
You'll hear the singing too.
--Unknown

8. Choose the most appropriate title for this poem. Circle the correct answer choice

Ⓐ The Singing Shell
Ⓑ The Song
Ⓒ Sea Shells
Ⓓ Sea Shell Song

Challenge Yourself!

- **Multi-Step Problems**
- **Finding the Theme**

https://www.lumoslearning.com/a/dc4-3

Day 3

See Page 7 for Signup details

Day 4

1. Andrew has a chart containing the numbers 1 through 100. He is going to put an "X" on all of the multiples of 10 and a circle around all of the multiples of 4. How many numbers will have an "X", but will not be circled?

    Ⓐ 3
    Ⓑ 4
    Ⓒ 5
    Ⓓ 8

2. Which number is a multiple of 30?

    Ⓐ 3
    Ⓑ 6
    Ⓒ 60
    Ⓓ 50

3. Use the Venn diagram below to respond to the following question.

    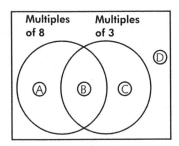

    In which region of the diagram would the number 72 be found?

    Ⓐ Region A
    Ⓑ Region B
    Ⓒ Region C
    Ⓓ Region D

4. Charlie has a chart containing the numbers 1 through 100. He is going to put an "X" on all of the multiples of 6 and a circle around all of the multiples of 8. Which of the following statements are correct? Choose all the correct answers.

    Ⓐ 12 numbers are circled.
    Ⓑ 9 numbers are circled but do not have X on them.
    Ⓒ 4 numbers are circled and also have X on them.
    Ⓓ 12 numbers have X on them but are not circled.

Mary walked quietly through the house so that she would not wake her parents. Before entering the kitchen, she stood and listened. She wanted to make sure that nobody had heard her and woken up. She slowly opened the cabinet door, trying to make sure that it didn't squeak. As Mary reached into the cabinet, something warm and furry touched her hand. Mary ran from the kitchen screaming loudly. Her father ran in to see what had happened. He started laughing when he saw their cat Purr Purr sitting quietly in the kitchen cabinet wagging her tail.

5. Choose the best summary of the above text.

Ⓐ Mary went to the kitchen. She stopped and listened. She opened the cabinet. She screamed. Her dad laughed.

Ⓑ Mary snuck quietly into the kitchen. When she opened the cabinet, something touched her hand and made her scream. Her dad came to help and discovered it was their cat in the cabinet.

Ⓒ The cat hid in the cabinet and scared Mary when she reached into it.

Ⓓ Mary walked into the kitchen after listening to make sure that nobody heard her. She opened the cabinet slowly and felt something touch her. She ran away screaming. She didn't know that it was her cat Purr Purr.

I was so scared when I first learned that I would be having my tooth pulled. I didn't sleep at all the night before the procedure. I was terrified that it would hurt more than I could tolerate. I was shaking when I sat in the dentist's chair. He promised me that it would not hurt, but I certainly had my doubts. The dentist gave me some medicine. When I awoke, my tooth was gone, and I didn't remember a thing.

6. Choose the best summary of the above text.

Ⓐ The writer was scared about having to have a tooth pulled and thought it would hurt. The dentist gave her medicine, and she didn't feel it when her tooth was pulled.

Ⓑ The writer was scared. She got her tooth pulled. The dentist gave her medicine.

Ⓒ The dentist gave the writer some medicine so that it wouldn't hurt when her tooth was pulled.

Ⓓ The writer was scared about having her tooth pulled. She didn't sleep the night before. She was terrified. She was shaking. The dentist gave her medicine. She didn't feel a thing when he pulled her tooth.

Huckleberry Hound ran through the yard and into the field next to his house. Suddenly, he put his nose to the ground and started sniffing as he walked. Yep, he definitely smelled a rabbit. He raised his head and howled loudly to let the other dogs know what he had found. Then, he shot after the rabbit like a bolt of lightning. He chased the rabbit for what seemed like hours, but he never caught it. He returned to his yard with his head hanging and his tail tucked between his legs.

7. Choose the best summary of the above text.

Ⓐ Huckleberry Hound smelled a rabbit. He chased it for a long time, but never caught it.

Ⓑ Huckleberry Hound smelled a rabbit. He ran across the yard to the field. He howled so the other dogs would know he found a rabbit. He shot after the rabbit and chased it for a long time. He didn't catch the rabbit. He went home with his head hung down.

Ⓒ Huckleberry Hound chased a rabbit.

Ⓓ Huckleberry Hound smelled a rabbit. He put his nose to the ground and followed its trail. He definitely smelled a rabbit. He chased it for a long time. He let the other dogs know he had found a rabbit. He didn't catch the rabbit.

Sam Walton

Sam Walton (1918-1992) founded Walmart and Sam's Club. He opened the first Wal-Mart Discount City in 1962 after having several franchise Ben Franklin stores. His main effort was to market American made products. Although after his death, this practice was not continued. He placed his stores close to distribution centers, thereby having stores in multiple areas, not just in major cities.

He was listed as the richest man in the US from 1982 to 1988. Walmart and Sam's Club stores operate in the US and in 15 other countries including, Canada, Japan, Mexico, and the UK.

8. Sam Walton tried to do which of the following with his stores? Circle the correct answer choice.

Ⓐ He tried to offer US made products in his chain of stores to help promote US made products and to help the country thrive.

Ⓑ Walton tried to have more stores than any other chain of discount stores.

Ⓒ Sam Walton offered his employees many days off and was never open on a holiday.

Ⓓ Sam Walton made sure that all of his stores were in major cities.

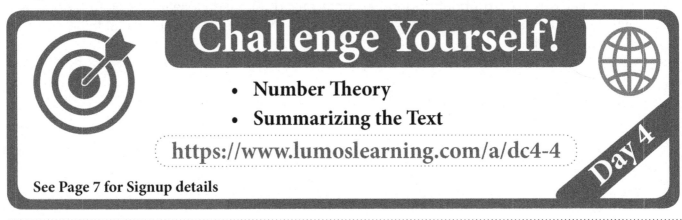

Challenge Yourself!

- **Number Theory**
- **Summarizing the Text**

https://www.lumoslearning.com/a/dc4-4

See Page 7 for Signup details

Day 4

Day 5

1. **Which of the following is not a true statement about the number sequence below?**
   26, 39, 52, 65, 78, 91

   Ⓐ The numbers are decreasing by 13.
   Ⓑ The sequence contains both even and odd numbers.
   Ⓒ The numbers are increasing by 13.
   Ⓓ The numbers are all multiples of 13.

2. **What would be the next three numbers in this pattern?**
   14, 21, 28, 35,

   Ⓐ 42, 50, 58
   Ⓑ 42, 49, 56
   Ⓒ 42, 49, 58
   Ⓓ 42, 48, 54

3. **Which of the following is not true of this pattern?**

   125,000; 150,000; 175,000; 200,000; 225,000

   Ⓐ The numbers are not descending.
   Ⓑ The numbers are all even.
   Ⓒ The numbers are increasing by 25,000.
   Ⓓ The numbers are all multiples of 50,000.

4. **Find the rule for this IN-OUT table. Circle the correct answer choice.**

IN	OUT
72	8
63	7
45	5

   Ⓐ Divide by 8
   Ⓑ Subtract by 56
   Ⓒ Subtract by 64
   Ⓓ Divide by 9

Timothy

Timothy is a student at my school. He is well-liked by all of the teachers and students. We all know that we can count on Timothy to keep our secrets, to help us if we ask, and to always be on time. We know that he is always honest and expects others to be honest as well.

Last summer, Timothy got a job walking dogs each morning. When school started this year, everyone encouraged him to quit his job, but he decided to keep it. He knew it would be hard to get up every morning at 5 a.m. in order to get all of the dogs walked and then go to school all day. Additionally, he planned to sing in the chorus, play basketball, and be a mentor in the tutoring program this year. He knows it will not be easy, but he thinks his hard work will be worth it. He is trying to save enough money to go to a youth camp next summer.

5. **According to the above passage, which set of adjectives would you choose to describe Timothy?**

Ⓐ responsible and depressed
Ⓑ trustworthy and thoughtless
Ⓒ responsible and ambitious
Ⓓ arrogant and unfriendly

6. **Based on the above passage, what do you think Timothy would do if someone asked him to help them cheat on a test?**

Ⓐ He would help them cheat but ask them not to tell anyone.
Ⓑ He would tell them that cheating is dishonest and encourage them not to do it.
Ⓒ He might help them cheat because he doesn't want them to make a bad grade.
Ⓓ He might tell them to ask someone else to help them cheat.

Fred Goes to the Dentist

Fred had never been to the dentist. All of his life he had heard horror stories about the buzzing drills, the huge needles, and the scary tools that the dentist used to torture his patients. Since none of his teeth were hurting, Fred just couldn't understand why his mom was insisting on taking him to the dentist. She told him that it was important to visit the dentist each year to have his teeth checked and cleaned. This seemed silly to Fred because he cleaned his teeth everyday by brushing and flossing them, but nothing would change his mother's mind. He found it hard to believe that she would think it was a good idea to take him somewhere to be tortured. However, he had no choice but to go.

On the way to the dentist, Fred's imagination went wild. He pictured walking into a room with a huge chair that the dentist would strap him to. He could just see the dentist pulling out a huge drill and drilling his tooth while his mother and several others held him in the chair. By the time he got to the dentist's office, he was shaking all over.

Surprisingly, the office was nothing like he expected. The dentist was friendly, and the chair was comfortable. It didn't have any straps. He looked around the room and didn't see any huge drills or torture devices. He was relieved when all the dentist did was look in his mouth, show him how to properly brush and floss his teeth, and give him a balloon. His mom made another appointment to have his teeth cleaned in six months. Maybe this wouldn't be as bad as he had thought it would be.

7. **Based on the passage, how do you think Fred felt about going to his first visit to the dentist?**

   Ⓐ He was excited and looked forward to it.
   Ⓑ He was afraid and didn't understand the reason he had to go.
   Ⓒ He was afraid but wanted to go and see the drills.
   Ⓓ He felt shy about meeting the dentist.

THE SECRET GARDEN by Frances Hodgson Burnett - Part 1
CHAPTER I
THERE IS NO ONE LEFT

When Mary Lennox was sent to Misselthwaite Manor to live with her uncle everybody said she was the most disagreeable-looking child ever seen. It was true, too. She had a little thin face and a little thin body, thin light hair and a sour expression. Her hair was yellow, and her face was yellow because she had been born in India and had always been ill in one way or another. Her father had held a position under the English Government and had always been busy and ill himself, and her mother had been a great beauty who cared only to go to parties and amuse herself with gay people. She had not wanted a little girl at all, and when Mary was born she handed her over to the care of an Ayah, who was made to understand that if she wished to please the Mem Sahib she must keep the child out of sight as much as possible. So when she was a sickly, fretful, ugly little baby she was kept out of the way, and when she became a sickly, fretful, toddling thing she was kept out of the way also. She never remembered seeing familiarly anything but the dark faces of her Ayah and the other native servants, and as they always obeyed her and gave her her own way in everything, because the Mem Sahib would be angry if she was disturbed by her crying, by the time she was six years old she was as tyrannical and selfish a little pig as ever lived. The young English governess who came to teach her to read and write disliked her so much that she gave up her place in three months, and when other governesses came to try to fill it they always went away in a shorter time than the first one. So if Mary had not chosen to really want to know how to read books she would never have learned her letters at all.

One frightfully hot morning, when she was about nine years old, she awakened feeling very cross, and she became crosser still when she saw that the servant who stood by her bedside was not her Ayah.

"Why did you come?" she said to the strange woman. "I will not let you stay. Send my Ayah to me."

The woman looked frightened, but she only stammered that the Ayah could not come and when Mary threw herself into a passion and beat and kicked her, she looked only more frightened and repeated that it was not possible for the Ayah to come to Missie Sahib.

There was something mysterious in the air that morning. Nothing was done in its regular order and several of the native servants seemed missing, while those whom Mary saw slunk or hurried about with ashy and scared faces. But no one would tell her anything and her Ayah did not come. She was actually left alone as the morning went on, and at last she wandered out into the garden and began to play by herself under a tree near the veranda. She pretended that she was making a flower-bed, and she stuck big scarlet hibiscus blossoms into little heaps of earth, all the time growing more and more angry and muttering to herself the things she would say and the names she would call Saidie when she returned.

"Pig! Pig! Daughter of Pigs!" she said, because to call a native a pig is the worst insult of all.

She was grinding her teeth and saying this over and over again when she heard her mother come out on the veranda with some one. She was with a fair young man and they stood talking together in low strange voices. Mary knew the fair young man who looked like a boy. She had heard that he was a very young officer who had just come from England. The child stared at him, but she stared most at her mother. She always did this when she had a chance to see her, because the Mem Sahib--Mary used to call her that oftener than anything else--was such a tall, slim, pretty person and wore such lovely clothes. Her hair was like curly silk and she had a delicate little nose which seemed to be disdaining things, and she had large laughing eyes. All her clothes were thin and floating, and Mary said they were "full of lace." They looked fuller of lace than ever this morning, but her eyes were not laughing at all. They were large and scared and lifted imploringly to the fair boy officer's face.

"Is it so very bad? Oh, is it?" Mary heard her say.

"Awfully," the young man answered in a trembling voice. "Awfully, Mrs. Lennox. You ought to have gone to the hills two weeks ago."

The Mem Sahib wrung her hands.

"Oh, I know I ought!" she cried. "I only stayed to go to that silly dinner party. What a fool I was!"

At that very moment such a loud sound of wailing broke out from the servants' quarters that she clutched the young man's arm, and Mary stood shivering from head to foot. The wailing grew wilder and wilder. "What is it? What is it?" Mrs. Lennox gasped.

"Some one has died," answered the boy officer. "You did not say it had broken out among your servants."

"I did not know!" the Mem Sahib cried. "Come with me! Come with me!" and she turned and ran into the house.

8. The passage describes Mary's characteristics and behavior. Mark all that apply.

- Ⓐ Mary was a sweet quiet child and quite agreeable.
- Ⓑ Mary was very spoiled by the servants and selfish.
- Ⓒ Mary was ill-tempered and tyrannical.
- Ⓓ All of the above.

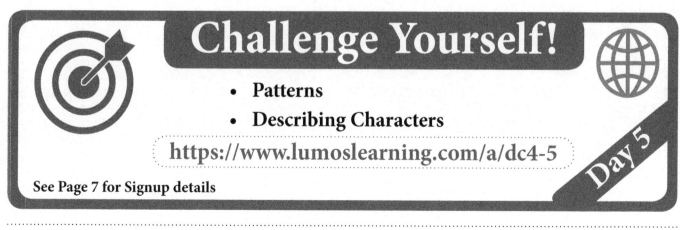

Challenge Yourself!

- **Patterns**
- **Describing Characters**

https://www.lumoslearning.com/a/dc4-5

Day 5

See Page 7 for Signup details

Learn Sign Language

What is American Sign Language?
American Sign Language (ASL) is a complete, complex language that employs signs made by moving the hands combined with facial expressions and postures of the body. It is the primary language of many North Americans who are deaf and is one of several communication options used by people who are deaf or hard-of-hearing.

Where did ASL originate?
The exact beginnings of ASL are not clear, but some suggest that it arose more than 200 years ago from the intermixing of local sign languages and French Sign Language (LSF, or Langue des Signes Française). Today's ASL includes some elements of LSF plus the original local sign languages, which over the years have melded and changed into a rich, complex, and mature language. Modern ASL and modern LSF are distinct languages and, while they still contain some similar signs, can no longer be understood by each other's users.

Source: https://www.nidcd.nih.gov/health/american-sign-language

Why should one learn sign language?

Enrich your cognitive skills: Sign language can enrich the cognitive development of a child. Since, different cognitive skills can be acquired as a child, learning sign language, can be implemented with practice and training in early childhood.

Make new friends: You could communicate better with the hearing-impaired people you meet, if you know the sign language, it is easier to understand and communicate effectively.

Volunteer: Use your ASL skills to interpret as a volunteer. volunteers can help in making a real difference in people's lives, with their time, effort and commitment.

Bilingual: If you are monolingual, here is an opportunity to become bilingual, with a cause.

Private chat: It would be useful to converse with a friend or in a group without anyone understanding, what you are up to.

Let's Learn the Alphabets

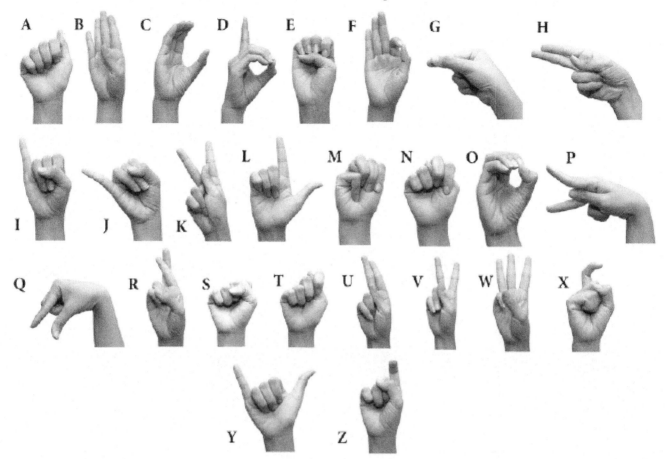

Sign language is fun if it is practiced with friends!
Partner with your friends or family members and try the following activities.

Activity

1. Communicate the following to your friend using the ASL.
   - USA
   - ASL

If your friend hasn't mastered the ASL yet, give the above alphabet chart to your friend.

2. Try saying your name in ASL using the hand gestures.

3. Have your friend communicate a funny word using ASL and you try to read it without the help of the chart. List the words you tried below.

Let's Learn the Numbers

Activity:

1. Share your postal code through ASL to your friend.
2. Communicate your home phone number in ASL to your friend.

Let's Learn Some Words

RED

ORANGE

YELLOW

GREEN

PURPLE

BLUE

EAT

DRINK

MORE

PLEASE

THANK YOU

SORRY

This Week's Online Activities

- Reading Assignment
- Vocabulary Practice
- Write Your Summer Diary

https://www.lumoslearning.com/a/slh4-5

See Page 7 for Signup details

Weekly Fun Summer Photo Contest

Take a picture of your summer fun activity and share it on Twitter or Instagram

Use the **#SummerLearning** mention

@LumosLearning on Twitter or

@lumos.learning on Instagram

Tag friends and increase your chances of winning the contest

Participate and stand a chance to WIN $50 Amazon gift card!

Day 1

1. What number can be found in the ten-thousands digit of 291,807?

   (A) 9
   (B) 1
   (C) 2
   (D) 0

2. Consider the number 890,260.
   The 8 is found in the _____ place.

   (A) ten-thousands
   (B) millions
   (C) thousands
   (D) hundred-thousands

Place Value Chart

Hundred-billions	Ten-billions	Billions	Hundred-millions	Ten-millions	Millions	Hundred-thousands	Ten-thousands	Thousands	Hundreds	Tens	Ones

3. What number correctly completes this statement?
   9 ten thousands = _____ thousands

   (A) 90
   (B) 900
   (C) 9
   (D) 19

4. Select the correct value for each number.

	5	50	500
How many hundreds are in 500?	Ⓧ	○	○
How many tens are in 500?	○	Ⓧ	○
How many ones are in 500?	○	○	Ⓧ

Describing the Setting (RL.4.3)

Day 1

Alexander the Great

Nearly two thousand five hundred years ago, there lived a king called Alexander the Great. He was the son of Philip II of Macedonia. When Prince Alexander was a boy, a magnificent horse that was for sale was brought to the court of his father. The animal was to be sold for thirteen talents. Talents are ancient coins. Many were eager to buy the horse, but no one could get close enough to saddle the restless animal. He was wild and impossible to ride.

Alexander pleaded with his father to let him try. Realizing that the horse was terrified of its own shadow, he turned the horse towards the sun so that its shadow fell behind it. This calmed the horse, and the prince proudly rode away. Observing this, his father said, "My son, look for a kingdom worthy of your greatness. Macedonia is too small for you."

That is exactly what Alexander tried to do when he grew up. He fought many battles and always rode Bucephalus (that was the horse's name.) Friendship and trust grew between the man and is horse. When Bucephalus died of wounds received in battle, Alexander was heartbroken and deeply mourned the loss of his horse.

5. When did this story take place?

Ⓐ two thousand five hundred years ago
Ⓑ two hundred and fifty years ago
Ⓒ twenty five hundred years ago
Ⓓ It is happening now

Fred Goes to the Dentist

Fred had never been to the dentist. All of his life he had heard horror stories about the buzzing drills, the huge needles, and the scary tools that the dentist used to torture his patients. Since none of his teeth were hurting, Fred just couldn't understand why his mom was insisting on taking him to the dentist. She told him that it was important to visit the dentist each year to have his teeth checked and cleaned. This seemed silly to Fred because he cleaned his teeth everyday by brushing and flossing them, but nothing would change his mother's mind. He found it hard to believe that she would think it was a good idea to take him somewhere to be tortured. However, he had no choice but to go.

On the way to the dentist, Fred's imagination went wild. He pictured walking into a room with a huge chair that the dentist would strap him to. He could just see the dentist pulling out a huge drill and drilling his tooth while his mother and several others held him in the chair. By the time he got to the dentist's office, he was shaking all over.

Surprisingly, the office was nothing like he expected. The dentist was friendly, and the chair was comfortable. It didn't have any straps. He looked around the room and didn't see any huge drills or torture devices. He was relieved when all the dentist did was look in his mouth, show him how to properly brush and floss his teeth, and give him a balloon. His mom made another appointment to have his teeth cleaned in six months. Maybe this wouldn't be as bad as he had thought it would be.

6. The setting for the second paragraph of the above passage is probably:

Ⓐ the dentist's office
Ⓑ an automobile
Ⓒ Fred's home
Ⓓ school

Huckleberry Hound ran through the yard and into the field next to his house. Suddenly, he put his nose to the ground and started sniffing as he walked. Yep, he definitely smelled a rabbit. He raised his head and howled loudly to let the other dogs know what he had found. Then, he shot after the rabbit like a bolt of lightning. He chased the rabbit for what seemed like hours, but he never caught it. He returned to his yard with his head hanging and his tail tucked between his legs.

7. At the beginning of the story, where was Huckleberry Hound?

Ⓐ in the yard
Ⓑ in a field
Ⓒ on the porch
Ⓓ in his kennel

Going Mudding with Dad

Jeff and his dad love to go mudding on their four wheelers. Mudding is great fun, but can be dangerous! Jeff has his own four wheeler, too. It is not as massive as his dad's but can go fast and sling mud everywhere. Mudding has become a sport of sorts in the swamp country in Louisiana where they live. So picture this in your mind. A four wheeler with a kid on it going through muddy paths covered in moss and vines. The mud is thick and water is everywhere. Get the picture, if you like mud like they do, it is a blast. The object of mudding is to see who can go the fastest beat the other "mudders" while getting the most mud and filth on them, as well.

There are several things to remember and keep in mind when preparing to drive and while driving four wheelers through mud. First, never go out alone. Buddy up is the best policy. Always wear plenty of clothing. Jeff and his dad wear long sleeve shirts, jeans, and high top hunting boots.

Never go on a four wheeler without wearing a helmet for protection. Most of them have seat belts, so buckle up. Take water or a vitamin sports drink and a healthy snack with you. Keep a first aid kit in your four wheeler, too. If you are going out on a path that has several trails, take strips of cloth and tie on branches along the way to find your way back. Be sure to inspect your vehicle before going out. Check the basic like oil, gas, clean off any mud left before hand and make sure that your vehicle starts and stops when needed. While driving do not turn your four wheeler too sharp at any time as this could cause it to flip over. If the curve ahead of you looks sharp, slow down before you approach, or you might have an accident, as well. Safety is more important than winning or being the muddiest one out there!

Then hit the trails, have fun and enjoy the mud!

8. Review the list of tips on mudding and mark all that apply.

Ⓐ Do not worry about going out alone.
Ⓑ Buddy up, buckle up, and wear plenty of clothing.
Ⓒ Take a first aid kit, take water and snacks, mark your path and inspect your vehicle before going out.
Ⓓ Wear a helmet, slow down on sharp curves, and do not turn sharp.
    Do not take snacks or drinks with you.

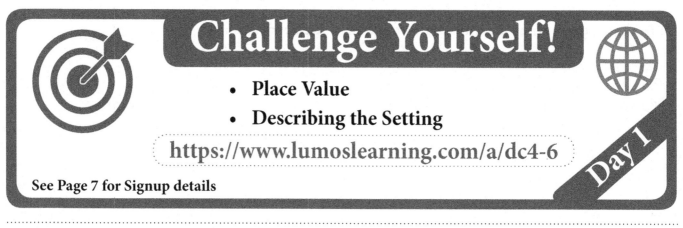

Challenge Yourself!

- **Place Value**
- **Describing the Setting**

https://www.lumoslearning.com/a/dc4-6

Day 1

See Page 7 for Signup details

Day 2

1. **Arrange the following numbers in ascending order.**
   62,894; 26,894; 26,849; 62,984

   Ⓐ 62,984; 62,894; 26,894; 26,849
   Ⓑ 26,894; 26,849; 62,984; 62,894
   Ⓒ 26,849; 62,984; 62,894; 26,894
   Ⓓ 26,849; 26,894; 62,894; 62,984

2. **Which of the following statements is true?**

   Ⓐ 189,624 > 189,898
   Ⓑ 189,624 > 189,246
   Ⓒ 189,624 < 189,264
   Ⓓ 189,624 = 189,462

3. **Which number will make this statement true?**
   198,888 > _____

   Ⓐ 198,898
   Ⓑ 198,879
   Ⓒ 198,889
   Ⓓ 199,888

4. **Compare the numbers then select <, >, or = to make the sentence true.**

	<	>	=
4,145 ___ 4,451	⊘	◯	◯
31,600 ___ 63,100	⊘	◯	◯
49 ___ 49	◯	◯	⊖
831 ___ 381	◯	⊘	◯

Timothy

Timothy is a student at my school. He is well-liked by all of the teachers and students. We all know that we can count on Timothy to keep our secrets, to help us if we ask, and to always be on time. We know that he is always honest and expects others to be honest as well.

Last summer, Timothy got a job walking dogs each morning. When school started this year, everyone encouraged him to quit his job, but he decided to keep it. He knew it would be hard to get up every morning at 5 a.m. in order to get all of the dogs walked and then go to school all day. Additionally, he planned to sing in the chorus, play basketball, and be a mentor in the tutoring program this year. He knows it will not be easy, but he thinks his hard work will be worth it. He is trying to save enough money to go to a youth camp next summer.

5. According to the above passage, Timothy is saving his money for what upcoming event?

Ⓐ a football game
Ⓑ a chorus trip
Ⓒ youth camp
Ⓓ a basketball game

6. Timothy gets up at 5 a.m. every morning to:

Ⓐ practice basketball
Ⓑ walk dogs
Ⓒ do his homework
Ⓓ tutor a classmate

Fred Goes to the Dentist

Fred had never been to the dentist. All of his life he had heard horror stories about the buzzing drills, the huge needles, and the scary tools that the dentist used to torture his patients. Since none of his teeth were hurting, Fred just couldn't understand why his mom was insisting on taking him to the dentist. She told him that it was important to visit the dentist each year to have his teeth checked and cleaned. This seemed silly to Fred because he cleaned his teeth everyday by brushing and flossing them, but nothing would change his mother's mind. He found it hard to believe that she would think it was a good idea to take him somewhere to be tortured. However, he had no choice but to go.

On the way to the dentist, Fred's imagination went wild. He pictured walking into a room with a huge chair that the dentist would strap him to. He could just see the dentist pulling out a huge drill and drilling his tooth while his mother and several others held him in the chair. By the time he got to the dentist's office, he was shaking all over.

Surprisingly, the office was nothing like he expected. The dentist was friendly, and the chair was comfortable. It didn't have any straps. He looked around the room and didn't see any huge drills or torture devices. He was relieved when all the dentist did was look in his mouth, show him how to properly brush and floss his teeth, and give him a balloon. His mom made another appointment to have his teeth cleaned in six months. Maybe this wouldn't be as bad as he had thought it would be.

7. Which detail shows that Fred is worried about going to the dentist?

Ⓐ "To his surprise, the office was nothing like he expected."
Ⓑ "Since none of his teeth were hurting, Fred just couldn't understand the reason that his mom was insisting on taking him to a dentist."
Ⓒ "By the time he got to the dentist he was shaking all over."
Ⓓ "Maybe this wouldn't be as bad as he thought it would be."

Disneyworld- Here We Come! Part - V

Again on the second day, we had the free breakfast and rode the trolley. It wasn't raining this time at all. Mom got out her map and we began our day. Daniel wanted to go back and ride the Mad Tea Party again, but thankfully Mom said no to that.

We were able to go to Splash Mountain, the Jungle Cruise, the 7 Dwarf's Mine Train and much more. Mom did make a request of her own. She wanted to meet Mickey and Minnie Mouse who were scheduled to appear outside of the Cinderella Castle. She also said she wanted to listen to the Enchanted Tales with Belle and ride the Prince Charming Regal Carrousel. What a crazy silly Mom!

What we didn't know was that she had a plan. It was right after we left the carrousel that we heard fantastic sounds coming down the main street. Yes, parade time right before our eyes. Mom told us to come and sit. There we were on the side of the castle sitting on the ledge in perfect view of the parade. We asked her how she knew to stop there. She said one of the hotel clerks had told her how to find the spot and when to be there. The parade was magnificent to say the least. The characters actually stopped in front of us and performed. Wow! We couldn't have planned it any better.

After the parade we went to A Pirate's Adventure and Tomorrowland Speedway, and Big Thunder Mountain. Mom said we needed to head toward the front entrance as it was time for fireworks and we needed to be ready. We got there just in time. The lights lit up the sky behind the Cinderella Castle and throughout Disneyworld. Just picture it!
What a perfect ending to our vacation

8. Explain the events that led up to them being able to see the parade from a wonderful view. Be sure to use details from the story to support your evidence. Write your answer in the box below.

thy city nut
houes and it was
thy purade

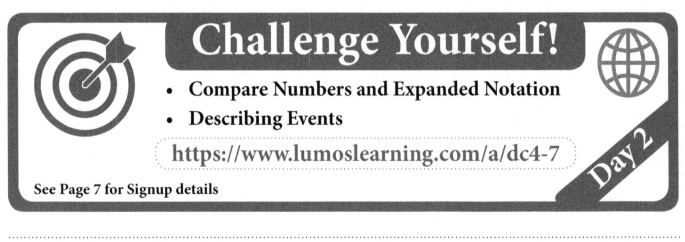

Challenge Yourself!

- **Compare Numbers and Expanded Notation**
- **Describing Events**

https://www.lumoslearning.com/a/dc4-7

Day 2

See Page 7 for Signup details

Day 3

1. **Round 4,170,154 to the nearest hundred.**

   Ⓐ 4,200,000
   Ⓑ 4,170,100
   Ⓒ 4,170,000
   Ⓓ 4,170,200

2. **Round 4,170,154 to the nearest thousand.**

   Ⓐ 4,200,000
   Ⓑ 180,000
   Ⓒ 4,170,000
   Ⓓ 4,179,200

3. **Round 4,170,154 to the nearest ten thousand.**

   Ⓐ 4,200,000
   Ⓑ 4,170,000
   Ⓒ 4,179,000
   Ⓓ 4,179,200

4. **This number 75,025 is rounded to the nearest ten thousand to get 760,000, List the possible digits that could go in the thousands place. Circle the correct answer.**

   Ⓐ 5,6,7,8,9
   Ⓑ 6,7,8,9
   Ⓒ 0,1,2,3,4
   Ⓓ 0,1,2,3,4,5

5. Identify the simile used in the below sentence.

Her eyes twinkled like diamonds as she looked lovingly at her new kitten.

Ⓐ her eyes twinkled
Ⓑ as she looked lovingly
Ⓒ at her new kitten
Ⓓ twinkled like diamonds

6. Identify the metaphor in the below sentence.

Elaine has no sympathy for others. You know she has a heart of stone.

Ⓐ no sympathy for others
Ⓑ a heart of stone
Ⓒ no sympathy
Ⓓ she has a heart

7. Identify the sentence that contains a metaphor.

Ⓐ She is as sweet as sugar.
Ⓑ She is as blind as a bat.
Ⓒ The sound of the chirping birds is music to my ears.
Ⓓ Billy is as stubborn as a mule.

GRAINS, GRAINS, GRAINS

Everyone knows that grains are an important healthy part of a good diet. It is important to make sure that you are eating the right number of grains daily.

To make sure this happens eat half of your diet in grains each day. Whole grain and wheat help to keep your digestive system in order and running smoothly, as well.

Did you know that whole grains and whole grain foods are made up of all three layers of the grain seed or kernel?

Here are the layers and explanations that will help you to understand.

1. The bran (outer layer): give you all of the fiber as well as B vitamins; minerals such as magnesium, iron and zinc, and some protein.

2. The endosperm (middle layer): makes up for most of the weight of the grain and is made up mainly of carbohydrate and protein.

3. The germ (inner layer): has B vitamins, unsaturated fats, vitamin E, and minerals.

Most whole grains are quite tasty such as brown rice, barley, whole oats or oatmeal, wheat and rye breads.

When you go shopping with your parents, do the healthy choice thing and read labels.

Whole grain foods will have the words 'whole' or 'whole grain' followed by the name of the grain as one of the first ingredients.

8. Match the term with it's definition

	germ (inner layer)	endosperm (middle layer)	bran (outer layer)
the weight of the grain	○	⊘	○
the fiber	○	○	⊘
unsaturated fats	⊘	○	○

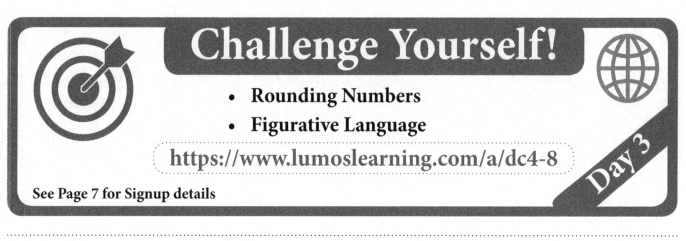

Challenge Yourself!

- **Rounding Numbers**
- **Figurative Language**

https://www.lumoslearning.com/a/dc4-8

See Page 7 for Signup details

Day 3

1. **What number acts as the identity element in addition?**

    Ⓐ 2-1
    Ⓑ 0
    Ⓒ 1
    Ⓓ None of these

2. **Which of the following number sentences illustrates the Commutative Property of Addition?**

    Ⓐ 3 + 7 = 7 + 3
    Ⓑ 9 + 4 = 10 + 3
    Ⓒ 11 + 0 = 11
    Ⓓ 2 + (3 + 4) = 2 + 7

3. **What number makes this number sentence true?**
    10 + ___ = 0

    Ⓐ 10
    Ⓑ $\frac{4}{10}$
    Ⓒ 0
    Ⓓ -10

4. **Find the sum: 4,927 + 5,098. Circle the correct answer.**

    Ⓐ 9025
    Ⓑ 9925
    Ⓒ 10,025
    Ⓓ 10,015

5. Which text structure is used in the classic story "The Three Little Pigs?"

Ⓐ Cause and effect
Ⓑ Compare and contrast
Ⓒ Problem and solution
Ⓓ Sequence

I saw the most unusual chair in a furniture store today while walking around the mall. The chair was shaped like a high-heeled shoe. The seat was created from the toe of the shoe, and the high heel and back of the shoe created the chair's back. Hot pink velvet covered the top portion of the chair. Black velvet covered the bottom and heel of the chair. Along the sides of the toes and heel, huge rhinestones were glued to the velvet. I wonder who would want this type of chair.

6. What is the structure of the above text?

Ⓐ Cause and effect
Ⓑ Compare and contrast
Ⓒ Problem and solution
Ⓓ Description

"Dad and I need to go out of town this weekend," said Mom. "We'll be back on Monday, so the three of you are going to spend the weekend with your two aunts. "

Lindsay, Scarlet, and Austin loved their aunts and were really excited. They ran upstairs and started getting their things together to take with them. They put everything in one bag that they would need for school. They were going to stay with Aunt Margaret for two nights and the last night with their Auntie Josephine.

At the end of the school day, the children came running out of classroom doors from all different directions. Aunt Margaret was waiting for her nieces and nephew at the entrance of the school. She was wearing a bright red suit with a sparkly cat pin on it. She also had on a proper wool hat to match. She noticed a scuff on her shoes when her nieces and nephew ran up to her.

She cried, "Oh, my goodness! I am so happy you are here. The children at your school are just a bunch of hooligans. I was nearly trampled while I was standing here! Let's get into the car." Aunt Margaret pointed to a large, green, four-door station wagon that was parked in the lot.

The next day, a funny-sounding honk came from the front of the house. The children ran outside and saw Auntie Jo sitting in her convertible. She was wearing a big cowboy hat. She wore a pair of polka dot shorts with a too large shirt.

7. What is the structure of the text?

Ⓐ a play
Ⓑ a comedy
Ⓒ a poem
Ⓓ a narrative

THE THREE GOLDEN APPLES, Part - 8

His nap had probably lasted a good while, when the cup chanced to graze against a rock, and, in consequence, immediately resounded and reverberated through its golden or brazen substance, a hundred times as loudly as ever you heard a church-bell. The noise awoke Hercules, who instantly started up and gazed around him, wondering whereabouts he was. He was not long in discovering that the cup had floated across a great part of the sea, and was approaching the shore of what seemed to be an island. And, on that island, what do you think he saw?

No; you will never guess it, not if you were to try fifty thousand times! It positively appears to me that this was the most marvelous spectacle that had ever been seen by Hercules, in the whole course of his wonderful travels and adventures. It was a greater marvel than the hydra with nine heads, which kept growing twice as fast as they were cut off; greater than the six-legged man-monster; greater than Antreus; greater than anything that was ever beheld by anybody, before or since the days of Hercules, or than anything that remains to be beheld, by travelers in all time to come. It was a giant!

But such an intolerably big giant! A giant as tall as a mountain; so vast a giant, that the clouds rested about his midst, like a girdle, and hung like a hoary beard from his chin, and flitted before his huge eyes, so that he could neither see Hercules nor the golden cup in which he was voyaging. And, most wonderful of all, the giant held up his great hands and appeared to support the sky, which, so far as Hercules could discern through the clouds, was resting upon his head! This does really seem almost too much to believe.

Meanwhile, the bright cup continued to float onward, and finally touched the strand. Just then a breeze wafted away the clouds from before the giant's visage, and Hercules beheld it, with all its enormous features; eyes each of them as big as yonder lake, a nose a mile Long, and a mouth of the same width. It was a countenance terrible from its enormity of size, but disconsolate and weary, even as you may see the faces of many people, nowadays, who are compelled to sustain burdens above their strength. What the sky was to the giant, such are the cares of earth to those who let themselves be weighed down by them. And whenever men undertake what is beyond the just measure of their abilities, they encounter precisely such a doom as had befallen this poor giant.

Poor fellow! He had evidently stood there a long while. An ancient forest had been growing and decaying around his feet; and oak-trees, of six or seven centuries old, had sprung from the acorn, and forced themselves between his toes.

8. **The narrator uses two sentences to intrigue and motivate the reader to go on. Choose the two sentences below from the passage that are evidence of this.**

Ⓐ And, on that island, what do you think he saw?
Ⓑ Poor fellow!
Ⓒ No; you will never guess it, not if you were to try fifty thousand times!
Ⓓ None of the above

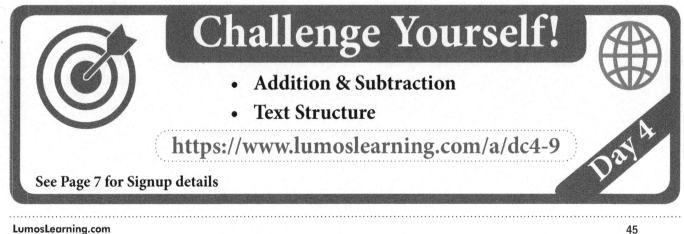

Day 5

1. Assume a function table has the rule "Multiply by 6." What would the OUT value be if the IN value was 8?

   Ⓐ 14
   Ⓑ 48
   Ⓒ 16
   Ⓓ 32

2. Solve.
   26 x 8 = ___

   Ⓐ 206
   Ⓑ 168
   Ⓒ 182
   Ⓓ 208

3. The number sentence 4 x 1 = 4 illustrates which mathematical property?

   Ⓐ The Associative Property of Multiplication
   Ⓑ The Identity Property of Multiplication
   Ⓒ The Distributive Property
   Ⓓ The Associative Property of Multiplication

4. The van traveled 1,458 miles every day from Monday through Friday. How many miles did it travel in all? Write your answer in the box below.

5. The below passage uses which style of narration?

You are not the kind of guy who would be at a place like this at this time of the morning. But here you are, and you cannot say that the terrain is entirely unfamiliar, although the details are fuzzy. —Opening lines of Jay McInerney's Bright Lights, Big City (1984)

Ⓐ First person
Ⓑ Second person
Ⓒ Third person
Ⓓ Fourth person

6. The below passage uses which style of narration?

I was so scared when I first learned that I would be having my tooth pulled. I didn't sleep at all the night before the procedure. I was terrified that it would hurt more than I could tolerate. I was shaking when I sat in the dentist's chair. He promised me that it would not hurt, but I certainly had my doubts. The dentist gave me some medicine. When I awoke, my tooth was gone, and I didn't remember a thing.

Ⓐ First person
Ⓑ Second person
Ⓒ Third person
Ⓓ Fourth person

7. The below passage uses which style of narration?

Huckleberry Hound ran through the yard and into the field next to his house. Suddenly, he put his nose to the ground and started sniffing as he walked. Yep, he definitely smelled a rabbit. He raised his head and howled loudly to let the other dogs know what he had found. Then, he shot after the rabbit like a bolt of lightning. He chased the rabbit for what seemed like hours, but he never caught it. He returned to his yard with his head hanging and his tail tucked between his legs.

Ⓐ First person
Ⓑ Second person
Ⓒ Third person
Ⓓ Fourth person

The Endangered Species Act.

The Act was originated in 1973, and is one of many US environmental laws passed in the 1970's. The law protects species from extinction. The United States Fish and Wildlife Service and the National Oceanic and Atmospheric Administration help to administer the act.

It was amended in 1978 to add economic considerations and again in 1982 which prevented economic considerations.

To be considered for listing, the species must meet one of five criteria (section 4(a)(1)):
1. There is the present or threatened destruction, modification, or curtailment of its habitat or range.
2. An over utilization for commercial, recreational, scientific, or educational purposes.
3. The species is declining due to disease or predation.
4. There is an inadequacy of existing regulatory mechanisms.
5. There are other natural or manmade factors affecting its continued existence.

8. In thinking about and considering types of endangered species, animals in particular, which one would you most be concerned with?

Which of the 5 listed criteria supports your concern? Write your answer in the box below.

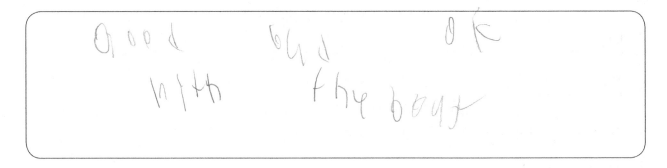

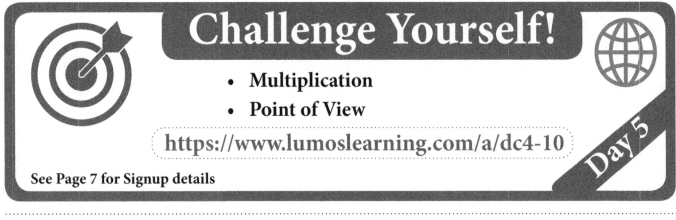

7 Tips to Improve Your Baseball Skills

Baseball, also known as "America's Pastime", is a sport that requires speed, strength, and focus.

When you first start learning baseball, one part of the game might be easier for you than others, but in order to be a great baseball player, it is important to be good at all aspects of the game. Below are seven tips to help you build upon your baseball skills and become a well-rounded player.

1. Practice Your Swing

The form and power of your swing must be correct to earn you hits and get on base. Even if you are very strong, you need the proper form in order to hit the ball.

Your form begins with a proper "athletic stance". An athletic stance means you are standing with your knees slightly bent and your shoulders directly over your feet.

Once your stance is set up, work on your swing. You might want to swing the bat as hard as you can, but don't forget to watch the ball, and follow your swing all the way through the plate.

Keep practicing your swing until it feels natural to you. Once you are making contact with the ball, you can start to swing the bat harder. If you add power gradually while always keeping your form in mind, you'll hit home runs in no time!

2. Improve Your Catch and Throw

When you are on defense, catching and throwing the ball is very important to getting the other team out and winning the game.

Your coach will likely have you catch and throw the ball at every practice, but consider working on these skills even when you're outside of practice.

Ask a teammate, friend, or even one of your parents to throw the ball around a few times per week. Your body will build "muscle memory", which means you will start to be able to throw and catch the ball more easily without even thinking about it.

3. Keep Your Eye On The Ball

A baseball field is very big, but the baseball itself is very small. This means you always need to know where the ball is and keep your eye on it when it comes to you.

When you're up to bat, remember to look closely at the ball to make hitting easier.

When you are in the outfield focus on the ball from when it is hit until it lands safely in your glove.

4. Build Your Speed

Throughout a baseball game, you will likely have to spring into action to either run to a base or run to field the ball.

If you don't work on your speed, it might feel like your legs are stuck in Jell-O when you try to sprint. Work on building your leg muscles by practicing short sprints to and from first base.

Practicing sprinting is not the most fun part of baseball, but it will truly make you a better player. You will be able to get more people out on defense, and score more often on offense!

5. Try Out Different Positions

There are many different positions in baseball so it can be hard to decide where you want to play.

While you might want to play the position you are naturally best at, you should try playing many different ones.

You may discover that you like a position more than you first thought. Additionally, you will have a competitive edge if you can play more than one position well.

6. Perfect Your Base Running

In order to score, you'll need to make it all the way around the bases. If you hit a home run, this is easy! However, most of the time you will probably be getting on base from hits.

You can get a little bit of a running start by taking a few steps past your base. Be careful, because the pitcher could try to get you out if you step too far from the base. If you build your speed enough and become very fast, your coach may even want you to "steal" a base. This means running to the next base while the pitcher isn't looking.

Next, pay attention to your teammate up to bat. If they hit the ball on the ground, you should run right away. If the ball is hit in the air, you should wait to see if the defensive player catches it before you begin running.

There are a lot of different rules in base running, so listen to the base coaches standing by first base and third base. They will tell you when to run and when to wait, and can help you improve your base running!

7. Practice Teamwork

Baseball is a sport that includes nine different players. This means that if you want to give your team the best chance at winning, you want every player on your team to be performing their best.

Learning a new sport can be hard, and when an entire team depends on you, you might be afraid of letting down your teammates. Help out other players by encouraging them to do their best, and letting them know that it is okay to make a mistake!

Teamwork should never be overlooked because after the game is over you will have a group of great friends to hang with!

This Week's Online Activities

- **Reading Assignment**
- **Vocabulary Practice**
- **Write Your Summer Diary**

https://www.lumoslearning.com/a/slh4-5

See Page 7 for Signup details

Weekly Fun Summer Photo Contest

Take a picture of your summer fun activity and share it on Twitter or Instagram

Use the **#SummerLearning** mention

@LumosLearning on Twitter or

@lumos.learning on Instagram

Tag friends and increase your chances of winning the contest

Participate and stand a chance to WIN $50 Amazon gift card!

1. **What role does the number 75 play in the following equation?**
   300 ÷ 75 = 4

   Ⓐ It is the dividend.
   Ⓑ It is the quotient.
   Ⓒ It is the divisor.
   Ⓓ It is the remainder.

2. **Which of the following division expressions will have no remainder?**

   Ⓐ 73 ÷ 9
   Ⓑ 82 ÷ 6
   Ⓒ 91 ÷ 7
   Ⓓ 39 ÷ 9

3. **Divide these blocks into 2 equal groups. How many will be in each group?**
   Note: 1 flat = 10 rods. 1 rod = 10 cubes

   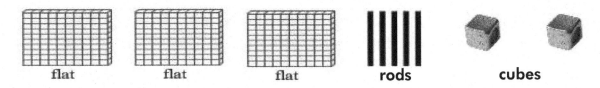

   | flat | flat | flat | rods | cubes |

   Ⓐ 352
   Ⓑ 176
   Ⓒ 152
   Ⓓ 132

4. **Complete the following table.**

Dividend	Divisor	Quotient	Remainder
128	8	16	0
435	7	62	1
350	6	58	2

"The Elephant Who Saw the World," Mary started speaking. It was Friday, and the students had to share their creative writing stories of the week.

Mary loved writing, and this part of the week, when they were able to make up stories for creative writing, was her favorite part. She enjoyed it so much that she became really good at it. When she was home on the weekends and she didn't have much homework, she would sit in her room for hours and create stories to share with her friends and family. Her parents always supported her and were her biggest fans.

However, there was one part about every Friday at school that Mary did not enjoy, and that was when she had to share her story in front of the class. The teacher made all of the children share on Friday afternoons, and this made Mary very nervous. She was shy, and although she knew her teacher was right, she didn't like it.

After sitting and listening to the other children's share, Mary finally heard her name called. She knew it was her turn to share. She got out of her seat slowly, walked to the front of the room and began.

5. Which picture below best represents what's happening in the story?

Ⓐ

Ⓒ

Ⓑ

Ⓓ None of the above

6. Which text below best represents what is happening in the picture?

Ⓐ Thelma watched her two baby lions, Louis and Lisa as they played. They were playing well until they started fighting over something the zoo keeper had thrown into the enclosure.

Ⓑ Thelma watched her two baby meerkats, Louis and Lisa, as they played. They were playing well until they started fighting over something the zoo keeper had thrown into the enclosure.

Ⓒ Thelma watched her two baby monkeys, Louis and Lisa, as they played. They were playing well until they started fighting over something the zoo keeper had thrown into the enclosure.

Ⓓ Thelma watched her two baby koala bears, Louis and Lisa, as they played. They were playing well until they started fighting over something the zoo keeper had thrown into the enclosure.

7. Which paragraph would be an appropriate description for the picture above?

Ⓐ One day last spring I was out walking as it was a beautiful spring day. I came across an empty forest and heard a noise. It sounded like a baby but it couldn't have been a baby since there was no one else there. I walked over to where I thought the noise was coming from and stopped in front of a large hollow tree. It looked as if it had been there for a very long time. I stopped and listened. I heard the noise again and it was definitely coming from inside the tree. I looked inside and I saw a little kitten.

Ⓑ One day last spring I was out walking as it was a beautiful spring day. I came across an empty parking lot and heard a noise. It sounded like a baby but it couldn't have been a baby since there was no one else there. I walked over to where I thought the noise was coming from and stopped in front of a large box. It looked like some thing someone may have used for moving. I stopped and listened. I heard the noise again and it was definitely coming from inside the box. I looked inside and I saw a little kitten.

Ⓒ One day last spring I was out walking as it was a beautiful spring day. I came across a construction site and heard a noise. It sounded like a baby but it couldn't have been a baby since there was no one else there. I walked over to where I thought the noise was coming from and stopped in front of a large cement pipe. It looked like some thing they might use to transport water underground. I stopped and listened. I heard the noise again and it was definitely coming from inside the pipe. I looked inside and I saw a little kitten.

Ⓓ At first the kitten was scared but eventually, with lots of coaxing, the kitten came to one of the open ends of the tree. I was able to see that it was a little black and white kitten who was probably very hungry and scared. I took the kitten home and it became my companion from that day on.

Sandy's Soccer

Sandy Thomas enrolled in soccer when she was in first grade. She had loved to watch the soccer games on TV with her dad. Sandy's dad was a high school soccer coach. It was his passion, as well as hers. Sandy was elated when she convinced her parents to let her play soccer rather than take ballet. Her friends were astonished as they had all signed up for ballet and expected her to, as well.

The team she was on this year was called, The Blue Jets. She was playing her favorite position, goalie. She practices at home with a goal her dad made for her. He tries to make the goal and she blocks it almost every time.

8. If the pattern stays exactly the same, what will game 3 score results be? Fill in the chart.

Game #	Team Blue Jets	Opposing Team	Difference + or -
1	10	8	+2
2	8	6	+2
3	10	8	+2

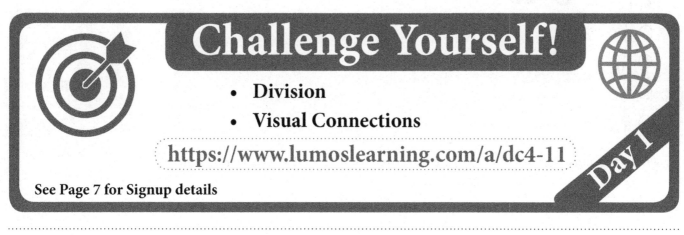

Challenge Yourself!

- **Division**
- **Visual Connections**

https://www.lumoslearning.com/a/dc4-11

Day 1

See Page 7 for Signup details

Day 2

1. **What fraction of these shapes are squares?**

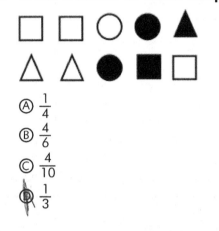

(A) $\frac{1}{4}$

(B) $\frac{4}{6}$

(C) $\frac{4}{10}$

(D) $\frac{1}{3}$

2. **What fraction of these shapes are not circles?**

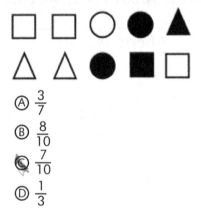

(A) $\frac{3}{7}$

(B) $\frac{8}{10}$

(C) $\frac{7}{10}$

(D) $\frac{1}{3}$

3. **What fraction of the squares are shaded?**

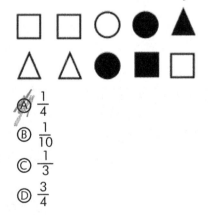

(A) $\frac{1}{4}$

(B) $\frac{1}{10}$

(C) $\frac{1}{3}$

(D) $\frac{3}{4}$

4. Write the simplest form of $\frac{120}{150}$. Write the answer in the box given below.

Fred Goes to the Dentist

Fred had never been to the dentist. All of his life he had heard horror stories about the buzzing drills, the huge needles, and the scary tools that the dentist used to torture his patients. Since none of his teeth were hurting, Fred just couldn't understand why his mom was insisting on taking him to the dentist. She told him that it was important to visit the dentist each year to have his teeth checked and cleaned. This seemed silly to Fred because he cleaned his teeth everyday by brushing and flossing them, but nothing would change his mother's mind. He found it hard to believe that she would think it was a good idea to take him somewhere to be tortured. However, he had no choice but to go.

On the way to the dentist, Fred's imagination went wild. He pictured walking into a room with a huge chair that the dentist would strap him to. He could just see the dentist pulling out a huge drill and drilling his tooth while his mother and several others held him in the chair. By the time he got to the dentist's office, he was shaking all over.

Surprisingly, the office was nothing like he expected. The dentist was friendly, and the chair was comfortable. It didn't have any straps. He looked around the room and didn't see any huge drills or torture devices. He was relieved when all the dentist did was look in his mouth, show him how to properly brush and floss his teeth, and give him a balloon. His mom made another appointment to have his teeth cleaned in six months. Maybe this wouldn't be as bad as he had thought it would be.

5. **Compare the way Fred felt about going to the dentist before his visit to the way he felt after his first visit.**

Ⓐ Fred was excited about going but became afraid once he arrived.
Ⓑ Fred was afraid of going and was even more afraid after he met the dentist.
Ⓒ Fred was afraid of going but felt relieved after he met the dentist.
Ⓓ Fred was excited about going and loved it once he arrived.

Passage 1:

Timothy

Timothy got a job walking dogs each morning. When school started this year, everyone encouraged him to quit his job, but he decided to keep it. He knew it would be hard to get up every morning at 5 a.m. in order to get all of the dogs walked and then go to school all day. Additionally, he planned to sing in the chorus, play basketball, and be a mentor in the tutoring program this year. He knows it will not be easy, but he thinks his hard work will be worth it. He is trying to save enough money to go to a youth camp next summer.

Passage 2:

Adam likes to spend time with his friends. If he is not with them, he is texting them or playing games with them online. Adam is always busy. He cannot stand to sit around and do nothing. In fact, the only time he is still is when he is sleeping. Adam plays football, basketball, soccer, and baseball. He loves to be involved in whatever is going on at school or at the town's youth center. He spends a lot of his time encouraging people to recycle and even volunteers at the youth center. Although he loves spending time with his friends, he is willing to give up time with them to help others.

Passage 3:

Stanley loves to stay at home. He enjoys activities that can be done alone such as reading, drawing, and spending time with his dogs. Most days after school you can find him at home enjoying one of his favorite activities. He also thinks recycling is important and makes sure his family does it. Although he likes being alone, he enjoys volunteering at the youth center with his brother. He thinks it is important to make a difference in the lives of others, which is why he thinks he would like to be a doctor. Adam and Stanley may be different in many ways, but they join together and make a difference in their community.

6. If you compare Timothy and Adam, which statement is correct?

- (A) Timothy participates in extracurricular activities, but Adam does not.
- (B) Timothy does not participate in extracurricular activities, but Adam does.
- (C) Timothy and Adam both participate in extracurricular activities.
- (D) Neither Timothy nor Adam participates in extracurricular activities.

7. If you contrast Timothy and Stanley, which statement is correct?

- (A) Stanley participates in many extracurricular activities such as sports and chorus, but Timothy does not.
- (B) Stanley and Timothy both participate in extracurricular activities such as sports and chorus.
- (C) Neither Stanley nor Timothy participates in extracurricular activities.
- (D) Stanley enjoys solitary activities such as drawing, but Timothy enjoys group activities such as chorus and sports.

GRAINS, GRAINS, GRAINS

Everyone knows that grains are an important healthy part of a good diet. It is important to make sure that you are eating the right number of grains daily.

To make sure this happens eat half of your diet in grains each day. Whole grain and wheat help to keep your digestive system in order and running smoothly, as well.

Did you know that whole grains and whole grain foods are made up of all three layers of the grain seed or kernel?

Here are the layers and explanations that will help you to understand.

1. The bran (outer layer): give you all of the fiber as well as B vitamins; minerals such as magnesium, iron and zinc, and some protein.
2. The endosperm (middle layer): makes up for most of the weight of the grain and is made up mainly of carbohydrate and protein.
3. The germ (inner layer): has B vitamins, unsaturated fats, vitamin E, and minerals.

Most whole grains are quite tasty such as brown rice, barley, whole oats or oatmeal, wheat and rye breads.

When you go shopping with your parents, do the healthy choice thing and read labels.

Whole grain foods will have the words 'whole' or 'whole grain' followed by the name of the grain as one of the first ingredients.

8. How can you help when you are out shopping with your parents to be sure healthy choices are made? Write your answer in the box below.

help your mom
pith saynen

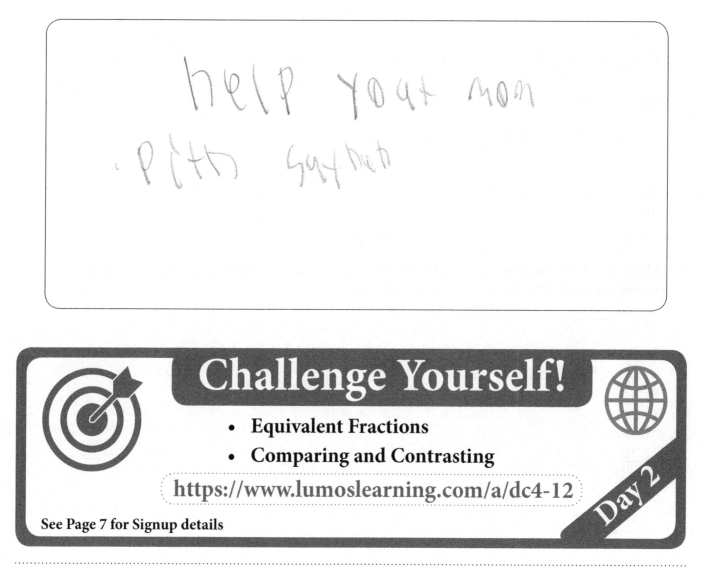

Challenge Yourself!

- **Equivalent Fractions**
- **Comparing and Contrasting**

https://www.lumoslearning.com/a/dc4-12

Day 2

See Page 7 for Signup details

Day 3

1. Where is Point D located on this number line?

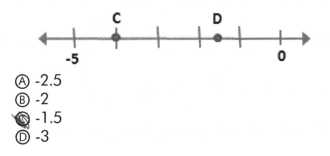

Ⓐ -2.5
Ⓑ -2
Ⓒ -1.5
Ⓓ -3

2. Which statement is true?

Ⓐ $\frac{4}{14} = \frac{6}{21} = \frac{8}{28}$

Ⓑ $\frac{4}{14} > \frac{6}{21} > \frac{8}{28}$

Ⓒ $\frac{4}{14} < \frac{6}{21} < \frac{8}{28}$

Ⓓ $\frac{4}{14} < \frac{6}{21} > \frac{8}{28}$

3. Compare the two fractions using < = or >:

    $\frac{3}{12} \underline{\qquad} \frac{3}{18}$

Ⓐ =
Ⓑ <
Ⓒ >

4. Which of the following fractions make this statement true? More than one answer maybe correct. Select all the correct answers

    $\frac{3}{5} > \underline{\qquad}.$

Ⓐ $\frac{4}{5}$

Ⓑ $\frac{3}{10}$

Ⓒ $\frac{8}{15}$

Ⓓ $\frac{12}{20}$

Day 3

The ostrich is the largest bird in the world, but it cannot fly. Its legs are so strong and long that it can travel faster by running. Ostriches use their wings to help them gather speed when they start to run. They also use them as brakes when turning and stopping.

Ostriches have been known to run at speeds of 60 miles per hour. This is faster than horses and matches the average speed of vehicles on a highway.

These huge birds stand as tall as horses and sometimes weigh as much as 298 pounds. In North Africa, they are often seen with other larger animals.

The zebra, which is also a fast runner, seems to be one of their favorite companions.

An ostrich egg weighs one pound, which is as much as two dozen chicken eggs. Ostrich eggs are delicious and are often used for food by people in Africa. The shells are also made into cups and beautiful ornaments.

5. Why is it a good thing that the Ostrich can run, rather than fly?

Ⓐ The Ostrich does not enjoy flying.
Ⓑ The Ostrich is able to fly.
Ⓒ The Ostrich does not want to fly.
Ⓓ The Ostrich can travel faster by running.

6. Devon says that Ostriches are shy and solitary birds. Which detail in the text proves him wrong?

Ⓐ "Ostrich eggs are delicious and are often used for food by people in Africa."
Ⓑ "An ostrich egg weighs one pound."
Ⓒ "These huge birds stand as tall as a horse."
Ⓓ "The zebra, which is also a fast runner, seems to be one of their favorite companions."

The blue whale is quite an amazing creature. It is a mammal that lives its entire life in the ocean. The size of its body is also amazing. This whale can grow up to 98 feet long and weigh as much as 200 tons. It is the largest known animal to have ever existed. Its body is long and elegantly tapered, unlike other whales which have a rounder, stockier build. The way that they are built, along with their extreme size, gives them a unique look. It also gives them the ability to move gracefully at greater speeds. Normally they travel around 12 mph, but they slow to 3.1 mph when feeding. They can even reach speeds up to 31 mph for short periods of time! Although they are extremely large animals, they eat small shrimp-like creatures called krill. Since the krill are so small, the blue whale eats about four tons daily as they swim deep in the ocean.

Blue whales do not live in tight-knit groups called pods like other whales. They live and travel alone or with one other whale. While traveling through the ocean, they come to the top to breathe air into their lungs through blowholes. They come from under the ocean, spitting water out of their blowholes. Then they roll and reenter the water with a grand splash of their large tails. They make loud, deep, and rumbling low-frequency sounds that travel great distances. This allows them to communicate with other whales as far as 100 miles away. Their cries can be felt as much as heard. This resonating call makes them the loudest animal on Earth. If you ever have the opportunity to see or hear a blue whale, it will be an experience you will not soon forget.

7. Angel argues that the blue whale is a solitary creature. What evidence from the text best supports his point?

Ⓐ "Blue whales do not live in tight-knit groups called pods like other whales. They live and travel alone or with one other whale."

Ⓑ "This whale can grow up to 98 feet long and weigh as much as 200 tons. It is the largest known animal to have ever existed."

Ⓒ "They make loud, deep, and rumbling low-frequency sounds that travel great distances. This allows them to communicate with other whales as far as 100 miles away."

Ⓓ "Although they are extremely large animals, they eat small shrimp-like creatures called krill."

2362 West Main Street
Jojo, TX 98456

June 16, 2017

Dear Mr. Seymour:

I ordered a Magic Racing Top from your company. The toy was delivered to me today in a package that was badly damaged. I took a picture of the box before I opened it, which I am sending to you as proof of the damage. The toy inside was broken due to the damage of the package during shipping.

This toy was to be a gift for my friend's birthday. There is not enough time before his party to wait for a replacement toy; therefore, I no longer need the toy. I would like for you to refund my money. Please send me a prepaid shipping label if you would like me to return the broken toy. Thank you for handling this matter for me. I look forward to hearing from you and hope we can satisfactorily resolve this problem.

Sincerely,
Tim West

8. Dominique argues that the writer of this letter was pleased with the toy company because he says, "please," and "if you would like." Does this evidence do a good job of supporting her argument? Circle the correct answer choice.

Ⓐ Yes. These are very polite words, so he is clearly pleased with the toy company.
Ⓑ Yes. He also says, "Thank you for handling this matter for me."
Ⓒ No. He is being polite, but he also says the package he ordered was, "badly damaged," and, "I would like for you to refund my money."
Ⓓ No. He wants to satisfactorily resolve the problem.

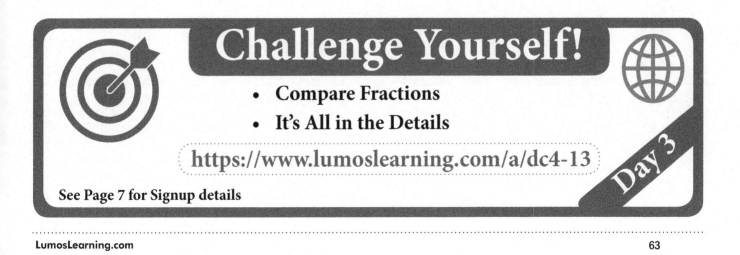

Challenge Yourself!

- Compare Fractions
- It's All in the Details

https://www.lumoslearning.com/a/dc4-13

Day 3

See Page 7 for Signup details

Day 4

1. **Find the sum:**

   $\frac{3}{12} + \frac{2}{12} =$

   Ⓐ $\frac{5}{24}$

   Ⓑ $\frac{6}{12}$

   Ⓒ $\frac{5}{12}$

   Ⓓ $\frac{1}{4}$

2. **Find the sum:**

   $\frac{2}{7} + \frac{1}{7} =$

   Ⓐ $\frac{3}{7}$

   Ⓑ $\frac{3}{14}$

   Ⓒ $\frac{2}{14}$

   Ⓓ $\frac{1}{3}$

3. **Use the following model to determine what fractional parts are shaded.**

   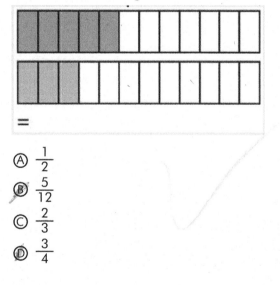

   $=$

   Ⓐ $\frac{1}{2}$

   Ⓑ $\frac{5}{12}$

   Ⓒ $\frac{2}{3}$

   Ⓓ $\frac{3}{4}$

4. Write $2\frac{5}{8}$ **as the sum of fractions. Select all the correct answers.**

Ⓐ $2 + \frac{3}{8} + \frac{2}{8}$

Ⓑ $1 + \frac{4}{8} + \frac{1}{8}$

Ⓒ $1 + 1 + \frac{4}{8} + \frac{1}{8}$

Ⓓ $1 + \frac{2}{3} + \frac{3}{5}$

The Main Idea (RI.4.2)

Day 4

The ostrich is the largest bird in the world, but it cannot fly. Its legs are so strong and long that it can travel faster by running. Ostriches use their wings to help them gather speed when they start to run. They also use them as brakes when turning and stopping.

Ostriches have been known to run at speeds of 60 miles per hour. This is faster than horses and matches the average speed of vehicles on a highway.

These huge birds stand as tall as horses and sometimes weigh as much as 298 pounds. In North Africa, they are often seen with other larger animals.

The zebra, which is also a fast runner, seems to be one of their favorite companions.

An ostrich egg weighs one pound, which is as much as two dozen chicken eggs. Ostrich eggs are delicious and are often used for food by people in Africa. The shells are also made into cups and beautiful ornaments.

5. What is the most appropriate title for this passage?

Ⓐ The Ostrich
Ⓑ The Bird that Cannot Fly
Ⓒ The Ostrich Egg
Ⓓ The Largest Bird in the World

6. What is the main idea of the passage?

(A) Ostriches are great because their eggs are delicious.
(B) The ostrich is the largest bird and can run very fast.
(C) The ostrich is the largest bird but it cannot fly.
(D) The ostrich lives in Africa.

Did you know that the coconut tree is very useful to people? Each part of the tree can be used for many different purposes. The coconut fruit, which we get from the tree, is very nutritious and is used to cook many foods. Coconut milk, which is taken from the coconut, tastes very delicious. It is used to prepare a variety of sweet dishes.

Oil can be extracted from a dried coconut. Coconut oil is a very good moisturizer. It is used in many beauty products like body wash, face wash, shampoos, and conditioners. The oil is also used for cooking of tropical foods. Some coconut trees grow straight and tall, and some trees are very short. Coconut trees do not have branches. They have long leaves which grow right at the top of the tree. The leaves have many different uses. Leaf ribs are made into brooms. The fiber obtained from the outer cover of the nut is used for mattresses and rugs. The trunk is used to make logs for small boats. It is also used for firewood. The sweet water of the tender coconut quenches thirst during the hot summer months and it is also very healthy.

7. What is the most appropriate title for this passage?

(A) The Coconut Tree and Its Uses
(B) Trees of the Rainforest
(C) Foods that We Get from the Coconut
(D) Tall Coconut Trees

Beatrice was so excited. This was truly a special day for her. She looked down and saw that her cup was sparkling with clean and cold water. She couldn't believe it was real as she had never seen water like that before. She slowly took a sip and it tasted so fresh. Her mother always told her how important water is.

The only way that Beatrice was able to get her water in the past was from the dirty water in a ditch not far from her home. Otherwise, they would have to walk for miles to reach other areas that had water. The water there wasn't very clean, either. In fact, most of the time, this water had a horrible smell and was brownish in color. Beatrice and her family knew it wasn't great but they didn't have any choice. The water that they drank from was contaminated making Beatrice feel sick often.

The water they mostly use is from streams, rivers, and lakes and is used for cooking, taking baths, and washing clothes. This water is contaminated from chemicals in the products they use and can cause diseases, such as typhus, cholera, dysentery, and malaria.

8. What would be the main idea of the story above?

Ⓐ Beatrice never had water that tasted so good before.
Ⓑ Beatrice is happy that she and her family will finally have clean drinking water.
Ⓒ Beatrice and her family get their water from the murky stream near the home.
Ⓓ Contaminated water often carries diseases and people can become very ill.

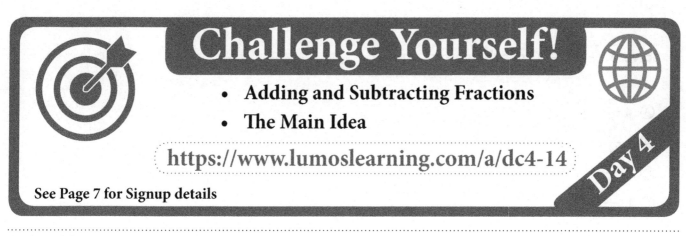

Challenge Yourself!

- **Adding and Subtracting Fractions**
- **The Main Idea**

https://www.lumoslearning.com/a/dc4-14

Day 4

See Page 7 for Signup details

Day 5

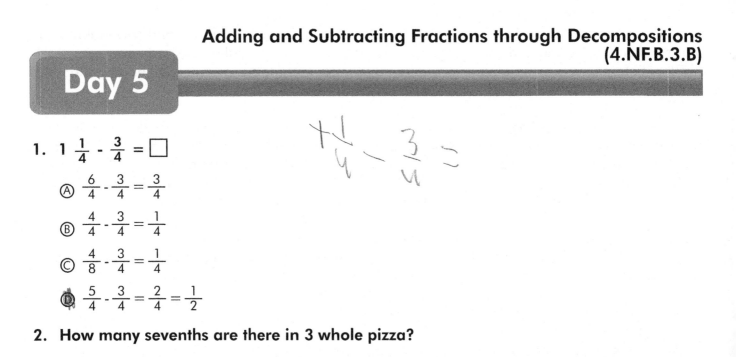

1. $1\frac{1}{4} - \frac{3}{4} = \square$

   Ⓐ $\frac{6}{4} - \frac{3}{4} = \frac{3}{4}$

   Ⓑ $\frac{4}{4} - \frac{3}{4} = \frac{1}{4}$

   Ⓒ $\frac{4}{8} - \frac{3}{4} = \frac{1}{4}$

   Ⓓ $\frac{5}{4} - \frac{3}{4} = \frac{2}{4} = \frac{1}{2}$

2. How many sevenths are there in 3 whole pizza?

   Ⓐ 7
   Ⓑ 14
   Ⓒ 28
   Ⓓ 21

3. What fractional part could be added to each blank to make each number sentence true?

   $\frac{3}{8} = \frac{1}{8} + \underline{\quad} + \underline{\quad}$;

   $\frac{3}{8} = \underline{\quad} + \frac{2}{8}$

   Ⓐ $\frac{2}{8}$

   Ⓑ $\frac{1}{8}$

   Ⓒ $\frac{0}{8}$

   Ⓓ $\frac{3}{8}$

4. Solve $8\frac{1}{2} - 4\frac{3}{4}$. Circle the correct answer.

   Ⓐ $4\frac{3}{4}$

   Ⓑ $3\frac{3}{4}$

   Ⓒ $3\frac{1}{4}$

   Ⓓ $4\frac{1}{4}$

Digestive System

The digestive system is made up of the esophagus, stomach, liver, gall bladder, pancreas, large and small intestines, appendix, and rectum. Digestion actually begins in the mouth when food is chewed and mixed with saliva. Muscles in the esophagus push food into the stomach. Once there, it mixes with digestive juices. While in the stomach, food is broken down into nutrients, good for you, and turned into a thick liquid. The food then moves into the small intestines where more digestive juices complete breaking it down. It is in the small intestines that nutrients are taken into the blood and carried throughout the body. Anything left over that your body cannot use goes to the large intestine. The body takes water from the leftovers. The rest is passed out of your body.

5. What event begins the digestive process?

- Ⓐ The small intestine absorbing nutrients.
- Ⓑ Muscles in the esophagus pushing food into the stomach.
- Ⓒ Chewing food and allowing it to mix with saliva.
- Ⓓ Nutrients are taken into the blood.

6. How do nutrients that are absorbed from food move through the body?

- Ⓐ They develop the ability to swim through the body's fluids in a tiny school bus.
- Ⓑ The digestive juices in the small intestine break them down.
- Ⓒ They move through the esophagus and into the stomach.
- Ⓓ They are absorbed into the blood, which carries them to other parts of the body.

The blue whale is quite an amazing creature. It is a mammal that lives its entire life in the ocean. The size of its body is also amazing. This whale can grow up to 98 feet long and weigh as much as 200 tons. It is the largest known animal to have ever existed. Its body is long and elegantly tapered, unlike other whales which have a rounder, stockier build. The way that they are built, along with their extreme size, gives them a unique look. It also gives them the ability to move gracefully at greater speeds. Normally they travel around 12 mph, but they slow to 3.1 mph when feeding. They can even reach speeds up to 31 mph for short periods of time! Although they are extremely large animals, they eat small shrimp-like creatures called krill. Since the krill are so small, the blue whale eats about four tons daily as they swim deep in the ocean.

Blue whales do not live in tight-knit groups called pods like other whales. They live and travel alone or with one other whale. While traveling through the ocean, they come to the top to breathe air into their lungs through blowholes. They come from under the ocean, spitting water out of their blowholes. Then they roll and reenter the water with a grand splash of their large tails. They make loud, deep, and rumbling low-frequency sounds that travel great distances. This allows them to communicate with other whales as far as 100 miles away. Their cries can be felt as much as heard. This resonating call makes them the loudest animal on Earth. If you ever have the opportunity to see or hear a blue whale, it will be an experience you will not soon forget.

7. How do blue whales breathe?

Ⓐ They use their blowholes to process oxygen found at deep ocean depths.
Ⓑ They spit water out of their blowholes and then rise to the surface to breathe air.
Ⓒ They rise to the surface, spit water out of their blowholes, and then breathe air in through their blowholes.
Ⓓ They roll and re-enter the water with a grand splash of their large tail.

There are many theories about how dinosaurs came to be extinct. Scientists do not all agree about what may have happened. The most recent idea says that a giant meteorite crashed into the earth. It kicked up enough dust and dirt that the Sun's rays did not reach Earth for a very long time. This prevented plants from making their own food via photosynthesis. Plant-eaters and then, meat-eaters died due to a lack of food.

The other leading idea says that dinosaurs died out when the Earth went through a time of volcanoes erupting. Like the meteorite idea, it is thought that the volcanoes spewed enough ash into the air that the Sun's rays were blocked. This also caused plant and animal life to die.

8. Do all scientists agree about how dinosaurs became extinct? Circle the correct answer choice.

Ⓐ No. The text explains that there are many theories on dinosaur extinction and describes two of them.
Ⓑ No. Some scientists believe dinosaurs died when a giant meteorite crashed into earth, while others blame extraterrestrials.
Ⓒ Yes. The scientific community has debated several possibilities, and they agree that dinosaurs died out as the result of widespread volcanic eruptions.
Ⓓ Yes. The scientists have argued but finally agree that they dinosaurs became extinct when a meteor crashed into Earth.

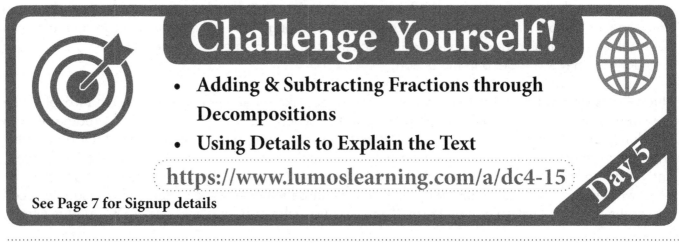

Challenge Yourself!

- **Adding & Subtracting Fractions through Decompositions**
- **Using Details to Explain the Text**

https://www.lumoslearning.com/a/dc4-15

Day 5

See Page 7 for Signup details

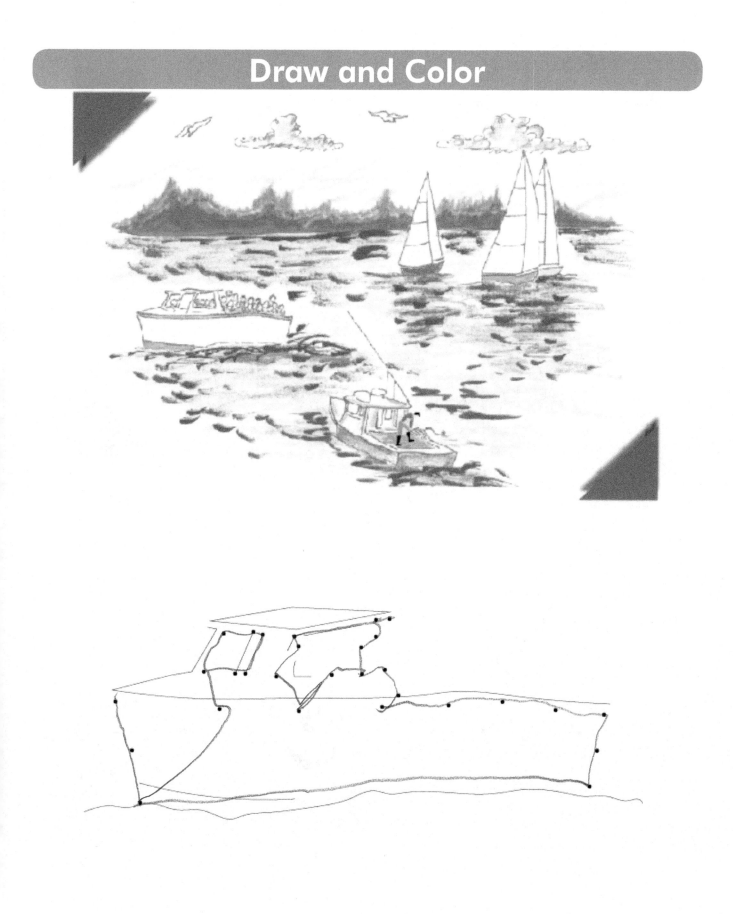

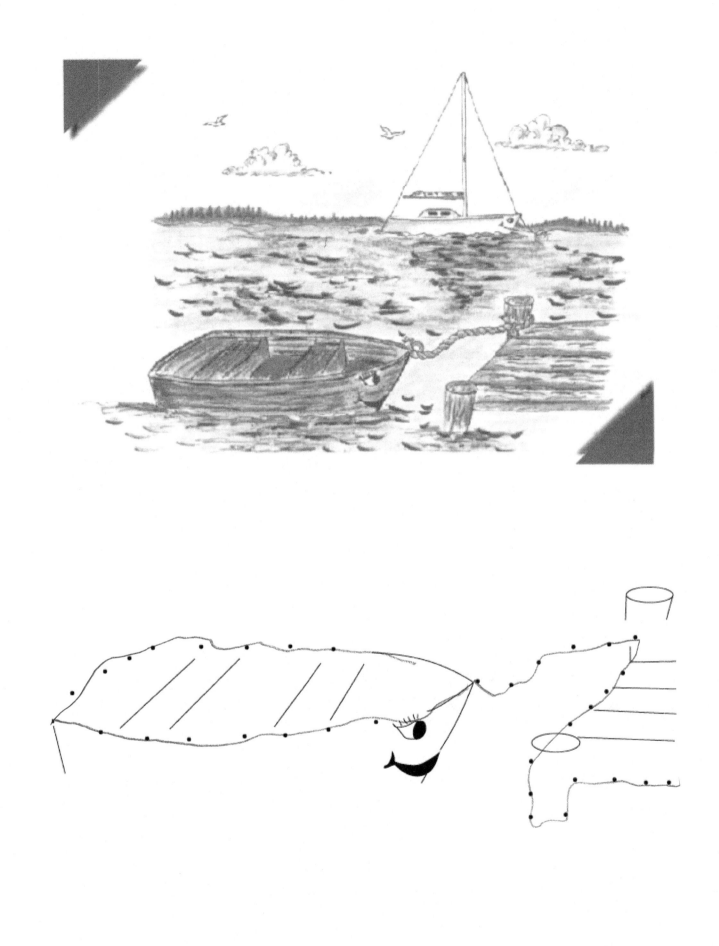

This Week's Online Activities

- **Reading Assignment**
- **Vocabulary Practice**
- **Write Your Summer Diary**

https://www.lumoslearning.com/a/slh4-5

See Page 7 for Signup details

Weekly Fun Summer Photo Contest

Take a picture of your summer fun activity and share it on Twitter or Instagram

Use the **#SummerLearning** mention

@LumosLearning on Twitter or

@lumos.learning on Instagram

Tag friends and increase your chances of winning the contest

Participate and stand a chance to WIN $50 Amazon gift card!

Day 1

Adding and Subtracting Mixed Numbers (4.NF.B.3.C)

1. Angelo picked $2\frac{3}{4}$ pounds of apples from the apple orchard. He gave $1\frac{1}{4}$ pounds to his neighbor Mrs. Mason. How many pounds of apples does Angelo have left?

   Ⓐ $1\frac{1}{2}$ pounds

   Ⓑ $1\frac{3}{4}$ pounds

   Ⓒ $2\frac{1}{4}$ pounds

   Ⓓ $1\frac{3}{8}$ pounds

2. Daniel and Colby are building a castle out of plastic building blocks. They will need $2\frac{1}{2}$ buckets of blocks for the castle. Daniel used to have two full buckets of blocks, but lost some, and now only has $1\frac{3}{4}$ buckets. Colby used to have two full buckets of blocks too, but now has $1\frac{1}{4}$ buckets. If Daniel and Colby combine their buckets of blocks, will they have enough to build their castle?

   Ⓐ No, they will have less than $1\frac{1}{2}$ buckets.

   Ⓑ No, they will have $1\frac{1}{2}$ buckets.

   Ⓒ Yes, they will have $2\frac{1}{2}$ buckets.

   Ⓓ Yes, they will have 3 buckets.

3. Lexi and Ava are making chocolate chip cookies for a sleepover with their friends. They will need $4\frac{1}{4}$ cups of chocolate chips to make enough cookies for their friends. Lexi has $2\frac{3}{4}$ cups of chocolate chips. Ava has $1\frac{3}{4}$ cups of chocolate chips. Will the girls have enough chocolate chips to make the cookies for their friends?

   Ⓐ They'll have less than 4 cups, but should just use the amount they have.

   Ⓑ They'll have less than 4 cups, so no.

   Ⓒ They'll have $4\frac{1}{4}$ cups, so yes.

   Ⓓ They'll have $4\frac{2}{4}$ cups, so yes.

4. Match each equation with the correct answer.

	$2\frac{2}{4}$	$3\frac{3}{4}$	$4\frac{1}{4}$
$2\frac{1}{4} + 1\frac{2}{4}$	○	⬤	○
$5\frac{1}{4} - 2\frac{3}{4}$	⬤	○	○
$2\frac{3}{4} + 1\frac{2}{4}$	○	○	⬤

What Does it Mean? (RI.4.4)

Day 1

The blue whale is quite an amazing creature. It is a mammal that lives its entire life in the ocean. The size of its body is also amazing. This whale can grow up to 98 feet long and weigh as much as 200 tons. It is the largest known animal to have ever existed. Its body is long and elegantly tapered, unlike other whales which have a rounder, stockier build. The way that they are built, along with their extreme size, gives them a unique look. It also gives them the ability to move gracefully at greater speeds. Normally they travel around 12 mph, but they slow to 3.1 mph when feeding. They can even reach speeds up to 31 mph for short periods of time! Although they are extremely large animals, they eat small shrimp-like creatures called krill. Since the krill are so small, the blue whale eats about four tons daily as they swim deep in the ocean.

Blue whales do not live in tight-knit groups called pods like other whales. They live and travel alone or with one other whale. While traveling through the ocean, they come to the top to breathe air into their lungs through blowholes. They come from under the ocean, spitting water out of their blowholes. Then they roll and reenter the water with a grand splash of their large tails. They make loud, deep, and rumbling low-frequency sounds that travel great distances. This allows them to communicate with other whales as far as 100 miles away. Their cries can be felt as much as heard. This <u>resonating</u> call makes them the loudest animal on Earth. If you ever have the opportunity to see or hear a blue whale, it will be an experience you will not soon forget.

5. What is the meaning of the word resonating?

Ⓐ low
Ⓑ loud
Ⓒ silent
Ⓓ quiet

Have you ever thought about what happened to the dinosaurs that once roamed the Earth? Well, scientists have developed several ideas throughout the years. One idea is that a giant meteorite crashed into our planet and caused a huge dust cloud to cover the Earth. The dust cloud was so enormous that it kept the sun's rays from reaching Earth. This caused all of the plants to die. With nothing to eat, the <u>herbivores</u> died. The large <u>carnivores</u> also died, leaving the planet without dinosaurs.

6. What is the meaning of the word herbivore?

Ⓐ a type of plant
Ⓑ an animal that eats only plants
Ⓒ a type of storm
Ⓓ an animal that eats only meat

7. What is the meaning of the word carnivores?

Ⓐ a type of plant
Ⓑ an animal that eats only plants
Ⓒ a type of storm
Ⓓ an animal that eats only meat

8. The first review of the Despicable Me was <u>favorable</u>. Many people attended and enjoyed the movie.
What is the meaning of the underlined word? Circle the correct answer choice.

Ⓐ clear
Ⓑ negative
Ⓒ positive
Ⓓ unsure

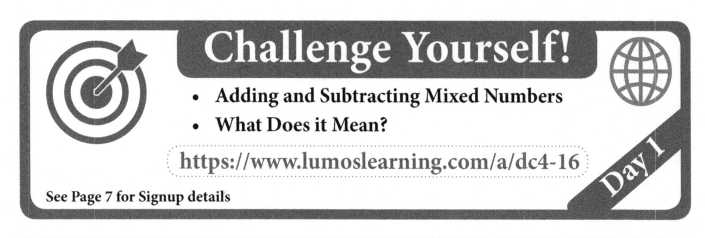

Challenge Yourself!

- **Adding and Subtracting Mixed Numbers**
- **What Does it Mean?**

https://www.lumoslearning.com/a/dc4-16

Day 1

See Page 7 for Signup details

Day 2

1. Marcie and Lisa wanted to share a cheese pizza together. Marcie ate $\frac{3}{6}$ of the pizza, and Lisa ate $\frac{2}{6}$ of the pizza. How much of the pizza did the girls eat together?

    Ⓐ $\frac{6}{6}$ of a pizza

    Ⓑ $\frac{5}{6}$ of a pizza

    Ⓒ $\frac{1}{2}$ of a pizza

    Ⓓ $\frac{4}{6}$ of a pizza

2. Sophie and Angie need $8\frac{5}{8}$ feet of ribbon to package gift baskets. Sophie has $3\frac{1}{8}$ feet of ribbon and Angie has $5\frac{3}{8}$ feet of ribbon. Will the girls have enough ribbon to complete the gift baskets?

    Ⓐ Yes, and they will have extra ribbon.

    Ⓑ Yes, but they will not have extra ribbon.

    Ⓒ They will have just enough ribbon to make the baskets.

    Ⓓ No, they will not have enough ribbon to make the baskets.

3. Travis has $4\frac{1}{8}$ pizzas left over from his soccer party. After giving some pizza to his friend, he has $2\frac{4}{8}$ of a pizza left. How much pizza did Travis give to his friend?

    Ⓐ $1\frac{1}{2}$ pizzas

    Ⓑ $1\frac{5}{8}$ pizzas

    Ⓒ $1\frac{3}{4}$ pizzas

    Ⓓ $1\frac{5}{7}$ pizzas

    $4\frac{9}{8} - 2\frac{4}{8} = 1\frac{5}{8}$

4. John and his friends ate $3\frac{1}{3}$ pizzas on Monday. They ate $2\frac{1}{4}$ pizzas on Tuesday. How much of the pizza did they eat in all? Select all the correct answers.

    Ⓐ $5\frac{7}{12}$ pizzas

    Ⓑ $5\frac{2}{7}$ pizzas

    Ⓒ $\frac{37}{7}$ pizzas

    Ⓓ $\frac{67}{12}$ pizzas

    $3\frac{1}{3} + 2\frac{1}{4} = 5\frac{}{}$

The blue whale is quite an amazing creature. It is a mammal that lives its entire life in the ocean. The size of its body is also amazing. This whale can grow up to 98 feet long and weigh as much as 200 tons. It is the largest known animal to have ever existed. Its body is long and elegantly tapered, unlike other whales which have a rounder, stockier build. The way that they are built, along with their extreme size, gives them a unique look. It also gives them the ability to move gracefully at greater speeds. Normally they travel around 12 mph, but they slow to 3.1 mph when feeding. They can even reach speeds up to 31 mph for short periods of time! Although they are extremely large animals, they eat small shrimp-like creatures called krill. Since the krill are so small, the blue whale eats about four tons daily as they swim deep in the ocean.

Blue whales do not live in tight-knit groups called pods like other whales. They live and travel alone or with one other whale. While traveling through the ocean, they come to the top to breathe air into their lungs through blowholes. They come from under the ocean, spitting water out of their blowholes. Then they roll and reenter the water with a grand splash of their large tails. They make loud, deep, and rumbling low-frequency sounds that travel great distances. This allows them to communicate with other whales as far as 100 miles away. Their cries can be felt as much as heard. This resonating call makes them the loudest animal on Earth. If you ever have the opportunity to see or hear a blue whale, it will be an experience you will not soon forget.

5. The author used which text structure when writing this passage?

- Ⓐ Problem and solution
- Ⓑ Cause and effect
- Ⓒ Sequence
- Ⓓ Descriptive

6. A report that explains how animal cells and plant cells are alike and how they are different would be written using which of the text structures?

- Ⓐ Cause and effect
- Ⓑ Compare and contrast
- Ⓒ Problem and solution
- Ⓓ Sequence or chronological

Grandma's Chocolate Cake
1 ¾ cups all-purpose flour
2 cups white sugar
2 sticks of room temperature butter
2 eggs
¾ cup cocoa powder
1 cup milk

1 tsp. vanilla extract
1 tsp. salt

Preheat oven to 350 degrees F.
Butter and flour two 8 inch cake pans.
Combine eggs, sugar, milk, vanilla extract, and butter. Beat until smooth.
Sift together the flour, salt, and cocoa powder.
Slowly add the sifted dry ingredients to the wet ingredients.
Mix until batter is smooth.
Pour the batter into the floured and greased cake pans.
Bake for 35 to 40 minutes.
Cool in pans on cooling rack for 30 minutes.
Ice cake with your favorite frosting.

7. Which text structure is used in the second half of the above recipe?

   Ⓐ Cause and effect
   Ⓑ Compare and contrast
   Ⓒ Problem and solution
   Ⓓ Sequence

8. If a title of an essay was "How I Spent My Summer Vacation," what type of writing would it be?

   Ⓐ Persuasive
   Ⓑ Informative
   Ⓒ Narrative
   Ⓓ Poetry

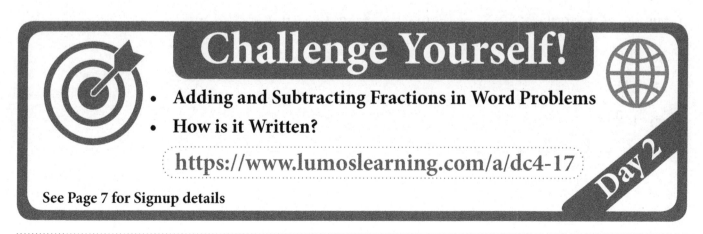

Challenge Yourself!

- Adding and Subtracting Fractions in Word Problems
- How is it Written?

https://www.lumoslearning.com/a/dc4-17

Day 2

See Page 7 for Signup details

Day 3

1. Solve $\frac{1}{2}$ x 6 =

   Ⓐ $\frac{2}{6}$

   Ⓑ $\frac{1}{3}$

   Ⓒ 3

   Ⓓ $\frac{3}{6}$

2. Solve 6 x $\frac{1}{4}$ =

   Ⓐ 2

   Ⓑ $1\frac{1}{2}$

   Ⓒ $\frac{4}{6}$

   Ⓓ 3

3. What product do these models show?

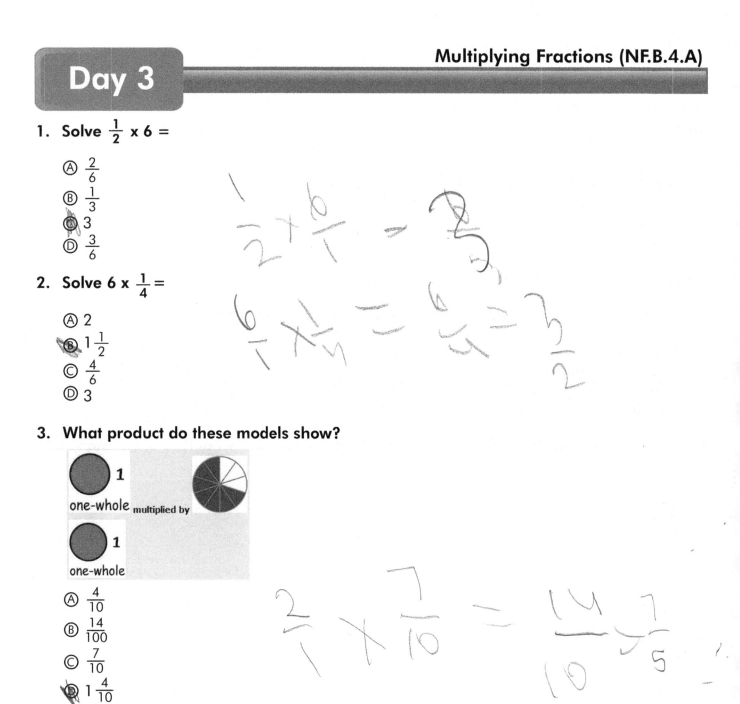

   Ⓐ $\frac{4}{10}$

   Ⓑ $\frac{14}{100}$

   Ⓒ $\frac{7}{10}$

   Ⓓ $1\frac{4}{10}$

4. Which of the following are equal to 5 x $\frac{2}{7}$. Select all the correct answers.

   Ⓐ $\frac{10}{7}$

   Ⓑ $\frac{2}{14}$

   Ⓒ $1\frac{3}{7}$

   Ⓓ $\frac{2}{7} + \frac{2}{7} + \frac{2}{7} + \frac{2}{7} + \frac{2}{7}$

The Parade: A Firsthand Account

When I got there I was dressed from head to toe in sparkly sequins and itchy tights, and I held my baton like a pro. I lined up with others in my squad and we began marching through the streets while the marching band played in front of us. I saw the crowds of people waving and smiling. At first, their happy faces made it seem less cold, but by the second mile the happy faces did not soothe the blisters on my feet. I threw my twirling baton into the air, and this time I did not catch it. In fact, when I turned to retrieve it, I tripped on the girl behind me and caused quite a situation. I was so embarrassed that I contemplated never showing my face again.

The Parade: A Secondhand Account

I read about the Thanksgiving parade in our school newspaper today. It was held downtown last Saturday morning to honor the American holiday that occurs every year on the third Thursday in November. There was a marching band, floats from all of the local businesses, a step team, a ballet studio, and baton twirlers. The temperature outside was forty five degrees, but the sun was shining brightly and helped warm over 600 people who came out to see the parade. All in all, the parade was a huge success, and the city plans to hold it again next year.

5. How is the focus of the firsthand account different from the secondhand account?

Ⓐ The firsthand account focuses on the parade itself, while the secondhand account focuses on the weather on the day of the parade.

Ⓑ The firsthand account has a wide focus that represents the parade as a whole, while the secondhand account is narrow and only talks about the crowd who attended the parade.

Ⓒ The firsthand account is more accurate, while the secondhand account is based on rumor.

Ⓓ The firsthand account focuses only on the personal experience of the speaker, while the secondhand account gives general information from the newspaper report about the parade.

6. How are the firsthand account and the secondhand account alike?

Ⓐ They both consider the parade a huge success.

Ⓑ They both give specific information about the number of people in attendance.

Ⓒ They both discuss the baton twirlers' sequin costumes.

Ⓓ They both discuss the weather, the marching band, the baton twirlers, and the crowd.

7. How are the firsthand account and the secondhand account different?

Ⓐ The firsthand account is more personal and includes the speaker's feelings about the parade, while the secondhand account is more objective and includes mostly facts about the parade.

Ⓑ The firsthand account includes more details about the parade, while the secondhand account is more of a broad summary.

Ⓒ The firsthand account is true, while the secondhand account gives false information.

Ⓓ The firsthand account discusses the origins of the parade, while the secondhand account is from a newspaper.

In the United States today, we are starting to see more and more of a problem with children who are overweight. Doctors and even the President's wife are trying to do something about it. They are recommending healthier foods and that children get daily exercise. They recommend that children go outside and do things instead of sitting in front of the tv. They have suggested that children get at least an hour of exercise a day by doing things like jumping rope or cycling, or anything else that makes their heart beat faster. This kind of exercise is known as aerobic exercise. They also recommend that children do exercises that strengthen the bones and muscles. There are lots of ways children can do this. Running is one example.

8. Which style of narration is used in the above text? Explain.

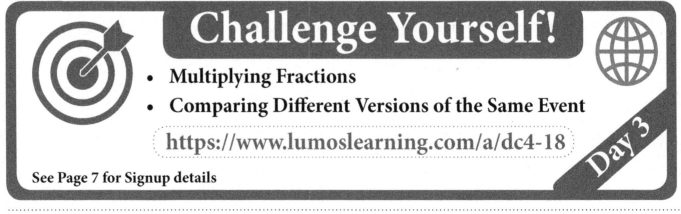

Day 4

1. $7 \times \frac{1}{3} =$

   Ⓐ $\frac{1}{21}$

   Ⓑ $\frac{3}{7}$

   Ⓒ $\frac{7}{22}$

   Ⓓ $\frac{7}{3}$

2. Cook is making sandwiches for the party. If each person at a party eats $\frac{2}{8}$ of a pound of turkey, and there are 5 people at the party, how many pounds of turkey are needed?

   Ⓐ 3 pounds

   Ⓑ $1\frac{1}{4}$ pounds

   Ⓒ $2\frac{1}{4}$ pounds

   Ⓓ $\frac{4}{8}$ pounds

   $\frac{2}{8} \times \frac{5}{1} = \frac{10}{8} = \frac{5}{4}$

3. $\frac{1}{5} \times 7 =$

   Ⓐ

   Ⓑ $\frac{7}{5}$

   Ⓒ $\frac{5}{7}$

   Ⓓ 35

   $\frac{1}{7}$

   $\frac{1}{5} \times \frac{7}{1} = \frac{7}{5}$

4. Fill in the missing number to complete the equation. $\frac{1}{2} \times \underline{\quad} = 4$

   8

There are four types of tissues that are created as cells join together and work as a group. Each type of tissue has a unique structure and does a specific job. Muscle tissue is made up of long, narrow muscle cells. Muscle tissue makes the body parts move by tightening and relaxing. Connective tissue is what holds up the body and connects its parts together. The bone is made up of connective tissue. Nerve tissue is made up of long nerve cells that go through the body and carry messages. Epithelial tissue is made of wide, flat epithelial cells. This tissue lines the surfaces inside the body and forms the outer layer of the skin. Groups of tissue join together to form the organs in the body such as the heart, liver, lungs, brain, and kidneys just to name a few. Then these organs work together to form the body systems. Each system works together, and with the other systems of the body.

Muscle Tissue	Connective Tissue	Nerve Tissue	Epithelial Tissue
- long, narrow cells - contracts and relaxes causing movement	- holds up the body - connects body parts together	- long cells - carries messages throughout the body	- wide, flat cells - lines inside surfaces - forms outer skin layer

5. How does the chart help the reader understand the functions of each of the four types of tissues?

Ⓐ It adds details not mentioned in the text so the reader can gather more information.
Ⓑ It elaborates on details mentioned in the text.
Ⓒ It changes some of the details mentioned in the text.
Ⓓ It clarifies the details mentioned in the text by categorizing them by tissue type.

6. Which types of tissue have similarly shaped cells?

Ⓐ epithelial tissue and connective tissue
Ⓑ muscle tissue and connective tissue
Ⓒ connective tissue and nerve tissue
Ⓓ muscle tissue and nerve tissue

7. To help the reader visualize what each tissue looks like, what would be the BEST visual aid to include with this text?

Ⓐ A drawing of the heart, liver, lungs, brain, and kidneys
Ⓑ A microscopic views of each type of tissue
Ⓒ A diagram of a nerve cell
Ⓓ A chart providing information about each type of tissue

Geologic Maps

As we all know, there are maps of many kinds. Most of us are familiar with maps that show us location of places, such as the map of the United States. However, other maps show other things. A geological map show where rocks and faults are at, as well as their location in an area. Then the map has various colors to show different information. It also includes many symbols. The geological map helps us to understand the earth beneath us, so we can understand the world around us better.

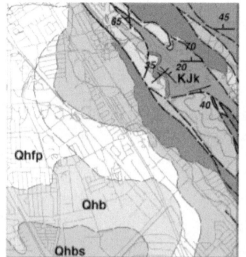

Notice the shaded areas on this map taken from the US Geological Survey website. Each area is colored to match the type of geological unit (volume of a certain kind of rock of a given age range). For example, one area might be colored bright orange to show a sandstone of one age while another might be pale brown to show another sandstone of a different age.

The geologists name and define the geological units they find. They determine everything they do based on their findings of rocks and the ages of the rocks. These continue to change as more investigations are completed. The science of geology can be quite interesting.

8. **In reading about geological maps and comparing that information to the information you know about the map of the United States.**
   Write a sentence in the box below explaining the differences in the types of maps.

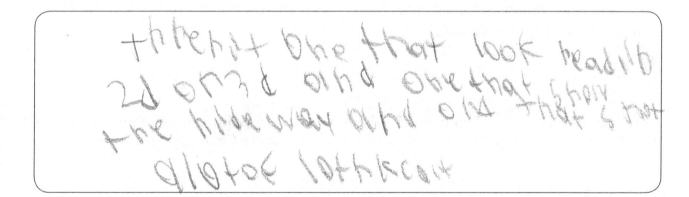

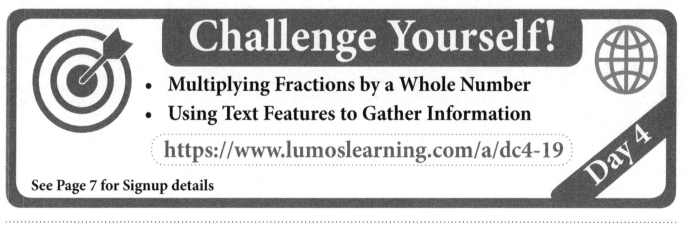

Day 5

1. Aimee is making treat bags for her Christmas party. She is going to put $\frac{2}{3}$ cups of mint M&Ms in each bag. She has invited 9 friends to her party. How many cups of mint M&Ms does she need for her friends' treat bags?

   Ⓐ 5 cups
   Ⓑ 6 cups
   Ⓒ 4 cups
   Ⓓ $5\frac{1}{2}$ cups

2. Aimee was making treat bags from Question #1, but then she decided to also include $\frac{1}{2}$ of a cup of coconut M&Ms in each bag. How many cups of coconut M&Ms does she need? (Remember that she has 9 friends.)

   Ⓐ $4\frac{1}{2}$ cups
   Ⓑ 4 cups
   Ⓒ $3\frac{1}{3}$ cups
   Ⓓ 3 cups

3. Aimee's mom bought palm tree bags to celebrate their move to Florida. This is their first Christmas in Florida. Each treat bag will hold one cup of treats. Aimee wants to use $\frac{2}{3}$ cup mint M&M's and $\frac{1}{2}$ cup coconut M&M's. Will Aimee be able to fit all of the M&Ms in each party bag for her friends?

   Ⓐ Yes
   Ⓑ No

4. John can paint $\frac{2}{5}$ of a table in 15 minutes. Jose can paint 8 times that amount in 15 minutes. How many tables can Jose paint in 15 minutes? Circle the correct answer.

   Ⓐ $2\frac{3}{5}$
   Ⓑ $\frac{1}{20}$
   Ⓒ $3\frac{2}{5}$
   Ⓓ $3\frac{1}{5}$

The blue whale is quite an amazing creature. It is a mammal that lives its entire life in the ocean. The size of its body is also amazing. This whale can grow up to 98 feet long and weigh as much as 200 tons. It is the largest known animal to have ever existed. Its body is long and elegantly tapered, unlike other whales which have a rounder, stockier build. The way that they are built, along with their extreme size, gives them a unique look. It also gives them the ability to move gracefully at greater speeds. Normally they travel around 12 mph, but they slow to 3.1 mph when feeding. They can even reach speeds up to 31 mph for short periods of time! Although they are extremely large animals, they eat small shrimp-like creatures called krill. Since the krill are so small, the blue whale eats about four tons daily as they swim deep in the ocean.

Blue whales do not live in tight-knit groups called pods like other whales. They live and travel alone or with one other whale. While traveling through the ocean, they come to the top to breathe air into their lungs through blowholes. They come from under the ocean, spitting water out of their blowholes. Then they roll and reenter the water with a grand splash of their large tails. They make loud, deep, and rumbling low-frequency sounds that travel great distances. This allows them to communicate with other whales as far as 100 miles away. Their cries can be felt as much as heard. This resonating call makes them the loudest animal on Earth. If you ever have the opportunity to see or hear a blue whale, it will be an experience you will not soon forget.

5. Which statement did the writer of this passage use to support his opinion that the size of a blue whale's body is amazing?

Ⓐ The blue whale is quite an extraordinary creature.

Ⓑ Its body is long and elegantly tapered, unlike other whales which have a rounder, stockier body.

Ⓒ This whale can grow up to 98 feet long and weigh as much as 200 tons, making it the largest known animal to have ever existed.

Ⓓ Their build, along with their extreme size, gives them a unique appearance and the ability to move gracefully and at greater speeds than one might imagine.

6. What evidence does the author provide in the second paragraph that supports the fact that whales communicate with one another?

Ⓐ Blue whales live and travel alone or with one other whale.

Ⓑ They emerge from the ocean, spewing water out of their blowhole, roll over, and re-enter the water with a grand splash of their tail.

Ⓒ They make loud, deep, and rumbling low-frequency sounds that travel great distances, which allow them to communicate with other whales as much as 100 miles away.

Ⓓ Their cries can be felt as much as heard.

Dr. Johnson thinks that everyone should take responsibility for preserving the toad species. By not mowing certain areas of our lawns, special areas of wild grass can be kept for toads. This practice may help to preserve the species. According to Dr. Johnson, dangerous chemicals found in pesticides and fertilizers are the reason that the toads are disappearing. The chemicals affect the food chain and kill the insects that toads eat. Dr. Johnson believes that the toads can be saved if we keep a space in our yards and stop using chemical fertilizers.

7. What would be an appropriate title for the above text?

Ⓐ Please Stop Mowing Your Lawn
Ⓑ Don't Let Toads Disappear
Ⓒ Please Stop Using Fertilizers
Ⓓ Dr. Johnson and the Toad

In the United States today, we are starting to see more and more of a problem with children who are overweight. Doctors and other health care professionals are trying to do something about it. They are recommending healthier foods and encouraging children get daily vigorous exercise. They also recommend that children go outside and play instead of sitting in front of the tv. They have suggested that children get at least an hour of exercise a day by participating in activities like jumping rope, cycling, or basketball, movement that makes the heart beat faster. This kind of exercise is known as aerobic exercise. Something else they recommend is for children to do exercises that strengthen the bones and muscles. There are a lot of ways that children can do this. One way is running.

8. What is the main idea of the above text? Circle the correct answer choice.

Ⓐ Doctors want you to move.
Ⓑ It is very important for kids to exercise daily.
Ⓒ Jumping and other activities help make bones strong.
Ⓓ Any physical exercise can help make the heart beat stronger.

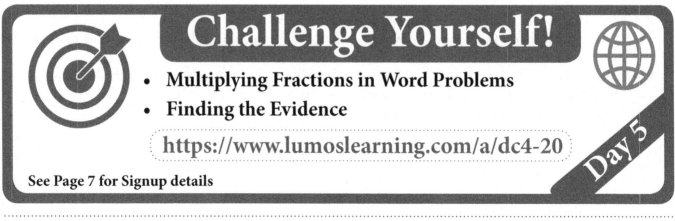

Challenge Yourself!

- **Multiplying Fractions in Word Problems**
- **Finding the Evidence**

https://www.lumoslearning.com/a/dc4-20

Day 5

See Page 7 for Signup details

Rock Out! Tips for Beginning Rock Climbers

When it comes to sports, rock climbing may not be the most common.

However, it's a fun, challenging, creative sport and a great way to be active!

We've got great tips for novice to intermediate climbers: if you're still early in your rock climbing career, focus on these important areas to improve your skills.

1. Join a rock climbing gym.

Rock climbing gyms offer clinics, classes, and the opportunity to boulder. Bouldering is a form or rock climbing where the walls are much shorter. Bouldering allows you to climb safely over a stretch of cushioned mat with no harness or ropes.

The ability to "free" climb means that you are able to develop the muscles in your hands, arms, and shoulders more than you would with the help of a harness and rope.

It's important to learn to climb inside and outside of a harness, in order to develop these muscles to their full potential, and bouldering is the only way to achieve that safely.

2. Overcome the fear of falling.

Clearly, you don't want to fall on purpose. However, a trained instructor will be able to hold you safely in your harness so that the ropes will catch you if and when you do fall.

Inevitably, there will be a course where you are forced to rely on your instructor to reach a new height or reach further than you would be able to without a harness.

In moments like these, trust your instructor, and communicate with them so that they know when and how to support you.

3. Relax your arms.

It's a natural tendency to want to bend your arms and hold your upper body close to the wall.

However, doing this is typically a mistake, one that can make you tired much faster! Practice holding on tightly with your hands but relaxing your arms, keeping them straight and allowing the force of your grip to hold you rather than your biceps.

You won't tire out as quickly and you will be able to climb for much longer without the muscles in your arms cramping.

4. Strengthen your core.

The term "core" refers to your abdominal muscles. While you might think about the muscles in your arms and shoulders in relation to climbing, you don't want to neglect the muscles in your core.

Think of your core muscles like the bridge connecting your lower and upper body: if the bridge is weak, the two ends won't stay even with each other, and you may lose your grip or footing.

Having a strong set of core muscles means that you are able to hold your abdomen tight, keeping your lower body still while you reach for a ledge.

Perform abdominal exercises like crunches, v kicks, and planks to strengthen these muscles.

5. Learn how to use chalk properly.

Chalk is used in many sports to keep sweat at bay. Sweaty hands make climbing slippery and difficult, which makes many climbers prone to over-chalking their hands in an effort to not slip.

However, too much chalk can be just as bad as not enough. Be sure to use just enough chalk to re-move extra sweat and moisture, but not so much that your hands are entirely caked.

Remember that you can always add more chalk as you go, but using too much chalk leaves extra on holds, and can make it harder for you to grip, rather than easier.

6. Nail the warm up.

Climbing takes a toll on a very specific group of muscles and tendons. Even though you use all of your muscles in climbing, the muscles in your upper body bear the brunt of the work!
Always start with a warm up, and don't rush it! Rushing through a warm up leaves you more likely to injure yourself, cramp, or tire faster than you would if your muscles are prepared to climb.

A good warm up includes exercises that gradually increase the circulation to your upper body: arm circles and upper body stretches are important to prime your body for climbing.

7. Focus on your weak side.

Most of us are left or right handed, and the dominant side of our bodies tends to be much stronger than the other. This muscle imbalance can make loving to the left more difficult to the right, or vice versa.

Work to strengthen both side of your body equaling by practicing climbs (while harnessed) that force to rely on your weaker side. This will help rebalance your strength and make you a more effective climber.

This Week's Online Activities

- **Reading Assignment**
- **Vocabulary Practice**
- **Write Your Summer Diary**

https://www.lumoslearning.com/a/slh4-5

See Page 7 for Signup details

Weekly Fun Summer Photo Contest

Take a picture of your summer fun activity and share it on Twitter or Instagram

Use the **#SummerLearning** mention

@LumosLearning on Twitter or

@lumos.learning on Instagram

Tag friends and increase your chances of winning the contest

Participate and stand a chance to WIN $50 Amazon gift card!

Day 1

10 to 100 Equivalent Fractions (4.NF.C.5)

1. **What fraction of a dollar is 6 dimes and 3 pennies?**
    Ⓐ 0.63 or $\frac{63}{100}$
    Ⓑ 0.73 or $\frac{73}{100}$
    Ⓒ 0.53 or $\frac{53}{100}$
    Ⓓ 0.43 or $\frac{43}{100}$

2. **1 tenth + 4 hundredths = _____ hundredths**

    Ⓐ 14
    Ⓑ 140
    Ⓒ 1400
    Ⓓ 104

3. **5 tenths + 2 hundredths = _____ hundredths**

    Ⓐ 25
    Ⓑ 525
    Ⓒ 52
    Ⓓ 502

4. **Match each fraction to it's equivalent.**

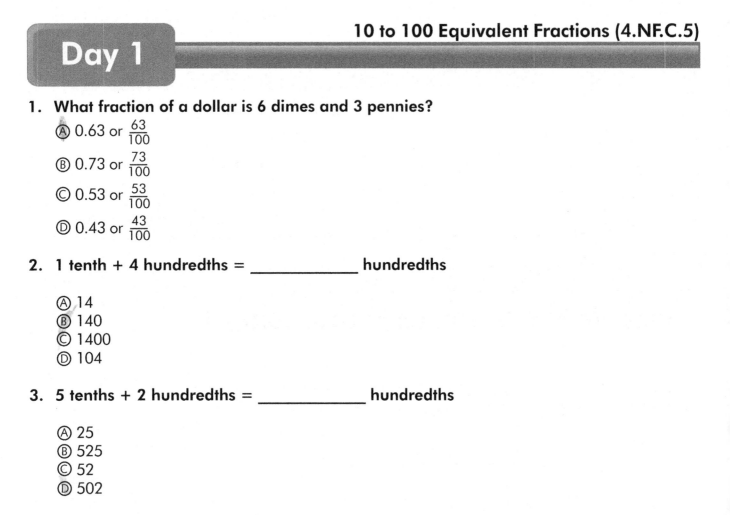

	$\frac{10}{100}$	$\frac{60}{100}$	$\frac{90}{100}$
$\frac{9}{10}$	○	○	⦿
$\frac{1}{10}$	⦿	○	○
$\frac{6}{10}$	○	⦿	○

On the Trail: an Outdoor Book for Girls by Adelia Beard and Lina Beard

For any journey, by rail or by boat, one has a general idea of the direction to be taken, the character of the land or water to be crossed, and of what one will find at the end. So it should be in striking the trail. Learn all you can about the path you are to follow. Whether it is plain or obscure, wet or dry; where it leads; and its length, measured more by time than by actual miles. A smooth, even trail of five miles will not consume the time and strength that must be expended upon a trail of half that length which leads over uneven ground, varied by bogs and obstructed by rocks and fallen trees, or a trail that is all up-hill climbing.

How to Camp Out by John M. Gould

Think over and decide whether you will walk, go horseback, sail, camp out in one place, or what you will do; then learn what you can of the route you propose to go over, or the ground where you intend to camp for the season. If you think of moving through or camping in places unknown to you, it is important to learn whether you can buy provisions and get lodgings along your route. See some one, if you can, who has been where you think of going, [Pg 10]and put down in a note-book all he tells you that is important.

5. Which sentence below integrates information from the above texts?

Ⓐ Hiking over bogs or fallen trees is harder than hiking an even, clear trail.
Ⓑ You should talk to someone who has been where you plan to go so you can get information and tips that will be helpful in planning your camping trip.
Ⓒ Hiking over uneven land will take longer than going the same distance over flat land.
Ⓓ When planning a camping trip, it is important to plan by considering both the type of the trail you will travel and whether you will walk or ride on horseback.

6. Which paragraph below combines information from the above texts?

Ⓐ Camping is terribly difficult, and only true experts should try to camp overnight.
Ⓑ If you plan to camp somewhere you've never been, you should learn everything you can about the trail. Find out what the land is like and where you can buy supplies along the way.
Ⓒ Only boys can go on long camping trips across bogs or uneven land.
Ⓓ You should always take a notebook on your camping trips to write about your trip and draw pictures of plants and animals you see.

7. Which pair of sentences shows similar information found in both texts?

Ⓐ "Learn all you can about the path you are to follow."
"Learn what you can of the route that you propose to go over."

Ⓑ "So it should be in striking the trail."
"Think over and decide whether you will walk, go horseback, sail, camp out in one place, or what you will do…"

Ⓒ "A smooth, even trail of five miles will not consume the time and strength that must be expended upon a trail of half that length which leads over uneven ground…"
"… It is important to learn whether you can buy provisions and get lodgings along your route."

Ⓓ All of the above

One Theory on Dinosaur Extinction

Have you ever thought about what happened to the dinosaurs that once roamed the Earth? Well, scientists have developed several ideas throughout the years. One idea is that a giant meteorite crashed into our planet and caused a huge dust cloud to cover the Earth. The dust cloud was so enormous that it kept the sun's rays from reaching Earth. This caused all of the plants to die. With nothing to eat, the herbivores died. The large carnivores also died, leaving the planet without dinosaurs.

Dinosaur Die-out: Competing Theories

There are many theories about how dinosaurs came to be extinct. Scientists do not all agree about what may have happened. The most recent idea says that a giant meteorite crashed into the earth. It kicked up enough dust and dirt that the Sun's rays did not reach Earth for a very long time. This prevented plants from making their own food via photosynthesis. Plant-eaters and then, meat-eaters died due to a lack of food.

The other leading idea says that dinosaurs died out when the Earth went through a time of volcanoes erupting. Like the meteorite idea, it is thought that the volcanoes spewed enough ash into the air that the Sun's rays were blocked. This also caused plant and animal life to die.

8. **Which of the following paragraphs integrates information from both of the above texts? Circle the correct answer choice.**

Ⓐ Dinosaurs are thought to have become extinct 65 million years ago, but some scientists theorize that they are still roaming remote parts of the Amazon Rainforest.

Ⓑ Dinosaurs became extinct because of widespread volcanic eruptions that blocked sunlight from reaching Earth. When this happened, plants died, beginning a disruption of the food chain that dinosaurs didn't survive.

Ⓒ One theory suggests a meteorite caused dinosaur extinction, while another claims widespread volcanic eruptions that caused the animals to die. Both theories, however, center around the idea that plants did not get needed sunlight and plant-eating and meat-eating animals died as a result.

Ⓓ None of the above

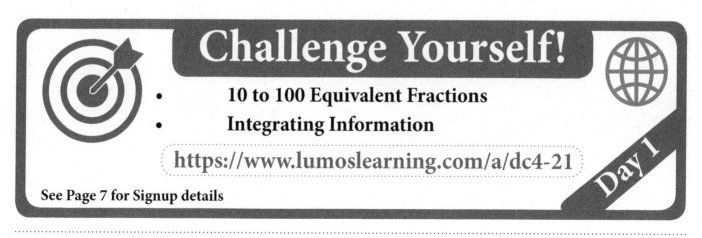

Challenge Yourself!

- **10 to 100 Equivalent Fractions**
- **Integrating Information**

https://www.lumoslearning.com/a/dc4-21

Day 1

See Page 7 for Signup details

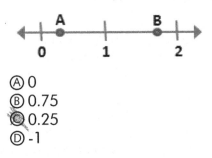

Day 2

1. Point A is located closest to _____ on this number line?

    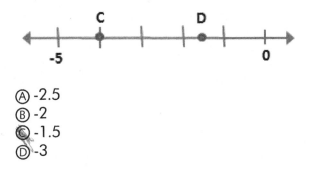

    Ⓐ 0
    Ⓑ 0.75
    Ⓒ 0.25
    Ⓓ -1

2. Convert $\frac{148}{1000}$ to a decimal.

    Ⓐ 0.148
    Ⓑ 14.8
    Ⓒ .00148
    Ⓓ 0.0148

3. Where is Point D located on this number line?

    Ⓐ -2.5
    Ⓑ -2
    Ⓒ -1.5
    Ⓓ -3

4. Which of the following numbers are equal to $\frac{6}{10}$? Select all the correct answers.

    Ⓐ 0.6
    Ⓑ 0.06
    Ⓒ $\frac{60}{100}$
    Ⓓ 0.60

5. Choose the correct pronoun to complete the sentence.

Bobby and I have practice every day. The 7th graders practice first and their practice always runs long. I live closer but Bobby is on my team, so ___ walk to the games together.

Ⓐ I
Ⓑ we
Ⓒ us
Ⓓ they

6. Choose the correct pronoun to complete the sentence.

My father asked me to bring ____ book inside.

Ⓐ he
Ⓑ him
Ⓒ his
Ⓓ us

7. Choose the correct pronoun to complete the sentence.

I would like you to meet Jamie. _____ is my best friend.

Ⓐ He
Ⓑ Him
Ⓒ Its
Ⓓ Their

8. Choose the appropriate pronoun. Fill in the blank by choosing the correct answer from the options given below.

_____ have been going to school together since first grade.

Ⓐ Them
Ⓑ He
Ⓒ Him
Ⓓ They

Challenge Yourself!

- **Convert Fractions to Decimals**
- **Pronouns**

https://www.lumoslearning.com/a/dc4-22

Day 2

See Page 7 for Signup details

Day 3

1. Point B is located closest to _____ on this number line.

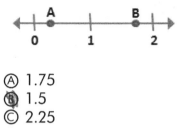

Ⓐ 1.75
Ⓑ 1.5
Ⓒ 2.25
Ⓓ 1.1

2. Compare the following decimals using <, >, or =.
   0.05 ___ 0.50

   Ⓐ 0.05 < 0.50
   Ⓑ 0.05 = 0.50
   Ⓒ 0.05 > 0.50

3. The rainbow trout dinner costs $23.99. The steak dinner costs $26.49. The roast chicken dinner is $5.00 less than $30.79. Which dinner costs the most?

   Ⓐ rainbow trout dinner
   Ⓑ steak dinner
   Ⓒ chicken dinner

4. Match the number pair with the correct inequality sign.

	<	>	=
0.25 _ 0.39	⊘	○	○
0.89 _ 0.890	○	○	⊘
0.12 _ 0.21	⊘	○	○
0.29 _ 0.28	○	⊘	○

5. Choose the correct progressive verb tense.
Efrain, accompanied by his parents, _____ to Europe this summer.

Ⓐ are traveling
Ⓑ will be traveling
Ⓒ was traveling
Ⓓ is traveling

6. Choose the correct verb to complete the sentence.
Darrel and I _____ the football game with friends this Friday night.

Ⓐ is attending
Ⓑ am attending
Ⓒ was attending
Ⓓ will attend

7. Choose the sentence that has the proper progressive verb tense.

Ⓐ Minnie, Jill, and Sandra are singing the birthday song to Ann right now.
Ⓑ Bob, Jim, and Harry have played baseball next summer.
Ⓒ One of my five hamsters might get out of the cage tomorrow night.
Ⓓ Twenty-five dollars are too much to charge for that bracelet.

8. Which verb best completes the sentence?
Kenji and Briana _____ at recess when their parents pick them up for their doctor appointments.

Ⓐ play
Ⓑ will play
Ⓒ will be playing
Ⓓ were playing

Day 4

1. **What customary unit should be used to measure the weight of the table shown in the picture below?**

    Ⓐ pounds
    Ⓑ inches
    Ⓒ kilograms
    Ⓓ tons

2. **Which of the following is an appropriate customary unit to measure the weight of a small bird?**

    Ⓐ grams
    Ⓑ ounces
    Ⓒ pounds
    Ⓓ units

3. **Complete the following statement:**
    A horse might weigh _____.

    Ⓐ about 500 pounds
    Ⓑ about 12 pounds
    Ⓒ about a gallon
    Ⓓ about 200 ounces

4. **Match each row with the correct conversion.**

	4	5	6
360 min = ___ hr	○	○	◉
500 cm = ___ m	○	◉	○
240 sec = ___ min	◉	○	○

5. Which sentences contains an auxiliary verb?

(1) Rae and her mother need to find a birthday gift for Rae's father, Joseph. (2) They discussed shopping online, walking to the store in their neighborhood, or going to the mall to find the gift. (3) Because Rae's mother suffers from arthritis, I don't think they will walk to the store to buy the gift. (4) They may decide it's most efficient to buy the gift online.

- Ⓐ sentence 1
- Ⓑ sentences 2 and 3
- Ⓒ sentence 4
- Ⓓ sentences 3 and 4

6. What is the purpose of the modal auxiliary verb, "may," in the sentence?
Oliver may go to school tomorrow if his fever has dissipated.

- Ⓐ It is being used to express doubt.
- Ⓑ It is being used to talk about a future event with uncertainty.
- Ⓒ It is being used to talk about something that will definitely happen.
- Ⓓ It is being used to talk about something that definitely will not happen.

7. Liam can have taken the test before he went on vacation, but he did not inform his teacher about the trip in advance.
Replace "can" with the correct verb in the sentence.

- Ⓐ will
- Ⓑ must
- Ⓒ can't
- Ⓓ could

8. What is the auxiliary modal verb in the sentence?
Dana had to leave the party when her mother called to inform her of an emergency at home.

- Ⓐ called to
- Ⓑ at
- Ⓒ had to
- Ⓓ will

Challenge Yourself!

- **Units of Measurement**
- **Modal Auxiliary Verbs**

https://www.lumoslearning.com/a/dc4-24

Day 4

See Page 7 for Signup details

Day 5

1. Arthur wants to arrive at soccer practice at 5:30 PM. He knows it takes him 42 minutes to walk to practice from his house. Estimate the time Arthur should leave his house to go to practice?

   Ⓐ 5:00 PM
   Ⓑ 4:45 PM
   Ⓒ 4:30 PM
   Ⓓ 3:45 PM

2. A baseball game began at 7:05 PM and lasted for 2 hours and 38 minutes. At what time did the game end?

   Ⓐ 9:43 PM
   Ⓑ 10:33 PM
   Ⓒ 9:38 PM
   Ⓓ 9:33 PM

3. 4 feet and 5 inches is the same as:

   Ⓐ 48 inches
   Ⓑ 53 inches
   Ⓒ 41 inches
   Ⓓ 65 inches

4. Sam was measuring out 6 cups of milk, but his measuring cup only measured 2 cups. How many times does he fill the measuring cup? Write your answer in the box below

5. Identify the _adverb_ used in <u>sentence 2</u>.
(1) Mary went to visit her grandmother last weekend. (2) She likes to visit her grandmother frequently. (3) While visiting, they enjoy walking. (4) They strolled in the beautiful park and talked. (5) Mary and her grandmother enjoyed their visit.

Ⓐ likes
Ⓑ visit
Ⓒ frequently
Ⓓ her

6. Identify the _adjective_ used in <u>sentence 4</u>.
(1) Mary went to visit her grandmother last weekend. (2) She likes to visit her grandmother frequently. (3) While visiting, they enjoy walking. (4) They strolled in the beautiful park and talked. (5) Mary and her grandmother enjoyed their visit.

Ⓐ strolled
Ⓑ beautiful
Ⓒ park
Ⓓ talked

7. Identify an _adjective_ in the below sentence.
Zelda and her family visited the Jackson Zoo last weekend although it was alarmingly cold and rainy.

Ⓐ last
Ⓑ although
Ⓒ and
Ⓓ cold

8. Fill in the blank using the correct adjective from the options given below.
It was determined that James was the _____ runner on our track team.

Ⓐ most fast
Ⓑ fastest
Ⓒ most fastest
Ⓓ faster

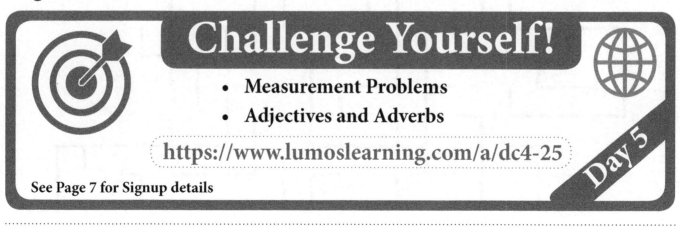

Challenge Yourself!

- **Measurement Problems**
- **Adjectives and Adverbs**

https://www.lumoslearning.com/a/dc4-25

Day 5

See Page 7 for Signup details

Maze Game

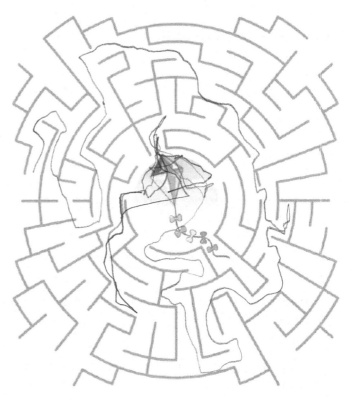

Help the beautiful kite fly out of the maze.

This Week's Online Activities

- **Reading Assignment**
- **Vocabulary Practice**
- **Write Your Summer Diary**

https://www.lumoslearning.com/a/slh4-5

See Page 7 for Signup details

Weekly Fun Summer Photo Contest

📷 Take a picture of your summer fun activity and share it on Twitter or Instagram

Use the **#SummerLearning** mention

@LumosLearning on Twitter 🐦 or

@lumos.learning on Instagram 📷

❮ Tag friends and increase your chances of winning the contest

Participate and stand a chance to WIN $50 Amazon gift card!

1. **A rectangular room measures 10 feet long and 13 feet wide. How could you find out the area of this room?**

   Ⓐ Add 10 and 13, then double the results
   Ⓑ Multiply 10 by 13
   Ⓒ Add 10 and 13
   Ⓓ None of the above

2. **A rectangle has a perimeter of 30 inches. Which of the following could be the dimensions of the rectangle?**

   Ⓐ 10 inches long and 5 inches wide
   Ⓑ 6 inches long and 5 inches wide
   Ⓒ 10 inches long and 3 inches wide
   Ⓓ 15 inches long and 15 inches wide

   48 feet

   Figure A   36 feet

3. **Which of these expressions could be used to find the perimeter of the above figure?**

   Ⓐ 48 + 36 + 2
   Ⓑ 48 x 36
   Ⓒ 2 x (48 + 36)
   Ⓓ 48 + 36

4. **What is the perimeter of the following 6 cm by 4 cm rectangle? Write the answer in the box given below.**

   6 cm

   4 cm

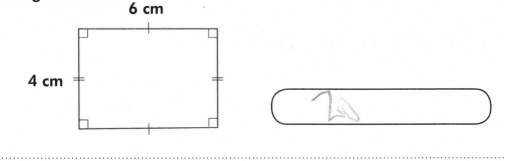

5. Choose the sentence that contains a prepositional phrase.

(A) The monkey was washing its paws.
(B) The lion jumped into the pool of cool water.
(C) That is the most beautiful dog I have ever seen.
(D) When you decide, let me know.

6. Identify the prepositional phrase in the below sentence.

You will find the new notebooks underneath the journals.

(A) will find
(B) notebooks underneath
(C) new notebooks
(D) underneath the journals

7. Choose the sentence that contains a prepositional phrase.

(A) Please put your paper down so that others won't see your answers.
(B) Because he doesn't have enough money to buy ice cream, he must do without.
(C) Do not leave for school without your lunch box.
(D) Please don't forget to let the dog in.

8. Which sentence does NOT contain a prepositional phrase? Circle the correct answer choice.

(A) I wish that my children wouldn't fight with each other.
(B) My little dog likes to sit on the couch.
(C) I will eat cereal for breakfast this morning.
(D) It is very hot outside today.

Challenge Yourself!

- **Perimeter & Area**
- **Prepositional Phrases**

https://www.lumoslearning.com/a/dc4-26

Day 1

See Page 7 for Signup details

1. The students in Mrs. Riley's class were asked how many cousins they have. The results are shown in the line plot. Use the information shown in the line plot to respond to the following. How many of the students have no cousins?

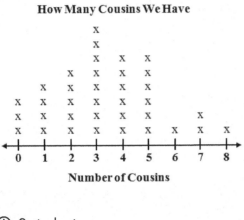

Ⓐ 0 students
Ⓑ 1 student
Ⓒ 2 students
Ⓓ 3 students

2. The students in Mrs. Riley's class were asked how many cousins they have. The results are shown in the line plot. Use the information shown in the line plot to respond to the following. How many of the students have exactly 4 cousins?

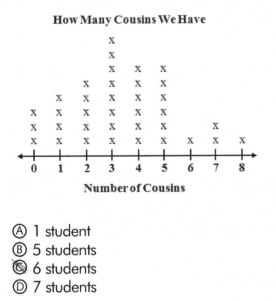

Ⓐ 1 student
Ⓑ 5 students
Ⓒ 6 students
Ⓓ 7 students

3. According to this graph, which are the 2 most favorite foods people enjoy at a carnival?

Favorite Carnival Foods

x			x			
x			x		x	x
x			x		x	x
x			x		x	x
x		x	x		x	x
x		x	x		x	x
x	x	x	x		x	x
x	x	x	x		x	x
x	x	x	x	x	x	x
x	x	x	x	x	x	x
x	x	x	x	x	x	x
caramel apples	elephant ears	corn dogs	cotton candy	french fries	candy apples	funnel cakes

Ⓐ candy apples and funnel cake
Ⓑ caramel apples and cotton candy
Ⓒ cotton candy and funnel cake
Ⓓ caramel apples and candy apples

4. Match each statement with the type of graph used for interpreting the data in each situation.

	Bar graph	Line graph	Pie Chart
The results of the number of boys in each grade.	○	○	○
The percentage of favorite desserts of the students in the class	○	○	○
The price of a car over the years.	○	○	○

5. Which answer choice corrects this run-on sentence?

Jordan wants to go outside and play with her neighbor her mother said she had to clean up her room first.

- Ⓐ Jordan wants to go outside and play with her neighbor, but her mother said she had to clean up her room first.
- Ⓑ Jordan wants to go outside and play but her mother won't let her.
- Ⓒ Jordan wants, to go outside and play with her neighbor but her mother said she had to clean up her room first.
- Ⓓ Jordan wants to go outside. And play with her neighbor. But her mother said she had to clean up her room first.

6. Which answer choice corrects the run-on sentence below?

George Washington Carver is best known for his work with peanuts but he also taught his students about crop rotation that's when farmers plant different crops each year to avoid draining the soil of its nutrients.

- Ⓐ George Washington Carver is best known for his work with peanuts, but he also taught his students about crop rotation, that's when farmers plant different crops each year to avoid draining the soil of its nutrients

- Ⓑ George Washington Carver is best known for his work with peanuts, but he also taught his students about crop rotation. That's when farmers plant different crops each year to avoid draining the soil of its nutrients.

- Ⓒ George Washington Carver is best known for his work with peanuts. But he also taught his students about crop rotation. That's when farmers plant different crops each year to avoid draining the soil of its nutrients

- Ⓓ George Washington Carver is best known for his work with peanuts but he also taught his students about crop rotation that's when farmers plant different crops each year to avoid draining the soil of its nutrients

7. Which answer choice is a fragment, rather than a complete sentence?

Ⓐ Be careful what you wish for.
Ⓑ He should not run with scissors.
Ⓒ If you can't say something nice.
Ⓓ Don't say anything at all.

8. What would transform this fragment into a complete sentence?

Three ways to transfer heat.

Ⓐ Replacing the period with a question mark at the end of the sentence
Ⓑ Adding "convection, conduction, and radiation" to the end of the sentence.
Ⓒ Adding "There are" to the beginning of the sentence.
Ⓓ Nothing. The sentence is complete already.

Challenge Yourself!
- Representing and Interpreting Data
- Complete Sentences

https://www.lumoslearning.com/a/dc4-27

Day 2

See Page 7 for Signup details

Day 3

1. In the figure below, two lines intersect to form ∠A, ∠B, ∠C, and ∠D. If ∠C measures 128°, then ∠A measures:

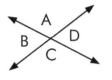

Ⓐ 52°
Ⓑ 128°
Ⓒ 90°
Ⓓ 180°

2. In the figure below, two lines intersect to form ∠A, ∠B, ∠C, and ∠D. If ∠C measures 128°, then ∠D measures:

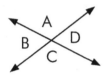

Ⓐ 52°
Ⓑ 128°
Ⓒ 90°
Ⓓ 180°

3. In the figure below, two lines intersect to form ∠A, ∠B, ∠C, and ∠D. If ∠B measures 68°, then ∠D measures:

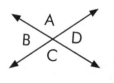

Ⓐ 152°
Ⓑ 90°
Ⓒ 180°
Ⓓ 68°

4. What is the angle measurement for the below angle? Type the number in the box.

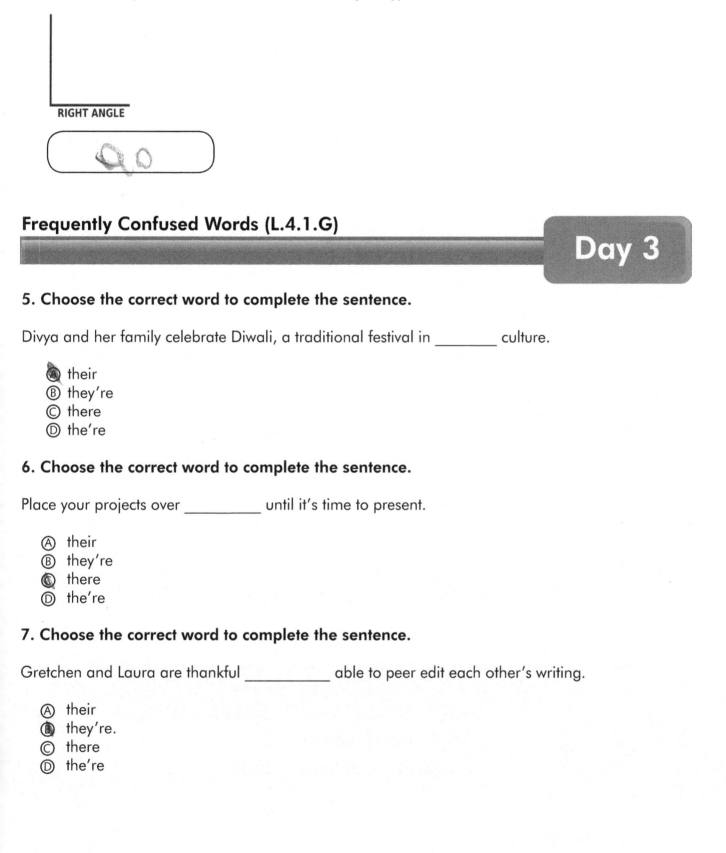

RIGHT ANGLE

90

Frequently Confused Words (L.4.1.G)

Day 3

5. Choose the correct word to complete the sentence.

Divya and her family celebrate Diwali, a traditional festival in _____ culture.

- Ⓐ their
- Ⓑ they're
- Ⓒ there
- Ⓓ the're

6. Choose the correct word to complete the sentence.

Place your projects over _____ until it's time to present.

- Ⓐ their
- Ⓑ they're
- Ⓒ there
- Ⓓ the're

7. Choose the correct word to complete the sentence.

Gretchen and Laura are thankful _____ able to peer edit each other's writing.

- Ⓐ their
- Ⓑ they're.
- Ⓒ there
- Ⓓ the're

8. Choose the correct sentence.

(A) We base our school rules around the common principal that everyone should be treated with respect.

(B) The principal called Evelyn to her office to reward her for perfect attendance.

(C) Jamar was extatic when he was chosen as a principle dancer in the ballet.

(D) Kelsey became the most principaled person at the school.

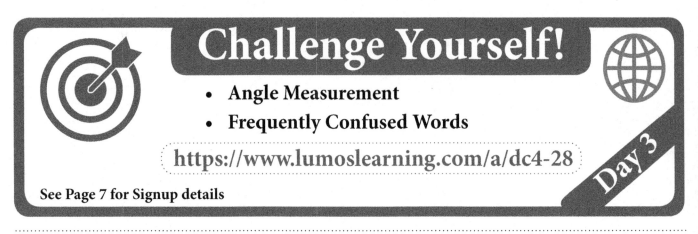

Challenge Yourself!

- Angle Measurement
- Frequently Confused Words

https://www.lumoslearning.com/a/dc4-28

See Page 7 for Signup details

Day 3

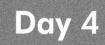

Day 4

1. At ice skating lessons, Erika attempts to do a 360 degree spin, but she only manages a half turn on her first attempt. How many degrees short of her goal was Erika's first attempt?

   Ⓐ 90 degrees
   Ⓑ 180 degrees
   Ⓒ 0 degrees
   Ⓓ 360 degrees

2. Erika's sister, Melanie, attempt to do a 360 degree turn, just like her sister, but she made a quarter turn on her first attempt. How many degrees short of her goal was Melanie's first attempt?

   Ⓐ 180 degrees
   Ⓑ 90 degrees
   Ⓒ 270 degrees
   Ⓓ 280 degrees

3. A water sprinkler covers 90 degrees of the Brown's backyard lawn. How many times will the sprinkler need to be moved in order to cover the full 360 degrees of the lawn?

   Ⓐ 4
   Ⓑ 2
   Ⓒ 3
   Ⓓ 5

4. When the measures of two angles A and B are added, you get 430 degrees. If the measure of angle A is 120degrees, what is the measure of angle B? Circle the correct answer

   Ⓐ 320°
   Ⓑ 310°
   Ⓒ 210°
   Ⓓ 550°

How is it Capitalized? (L.4.2.A)

Day 4

5. Identify the words that need to be capitalized in the below sentence.

Although spring and summer are my favorite seasons, our family gathering on thanksgiving makes november my favorite month.

- Ⓐ   Spring, November
- Ⓑ   Thanksgiving, November
- Ⓒ   Summer, Thanksgiving
- Ⓓ   Seasons, November

6 Part A

Correctly capitalize the underlined portion of the below address.

dr. j. howard smith
1141 east palm street
washington, la 98654

- Ⓐ   Dr. J. Howard Smith
- Ⓑ   DR. J. Howard Smith
- Ⓒ   Dr. J. howard smith
- Ⓓ   Dr. j. Howard Smith

Part B

Correctly capitalize the underlined portion of the below address.

dr. j. howard smith
1141 east palm street
washington, la 98654

- Ⓐ   1141 east Palm Street
- Ⓑ   1141 East palm Street
- Ⓒ   1141 east palm Street
- Ⓓ   1141 East Palm Street

7. Correctly capitalize the underlined portion of the below address.

dr. j. howard smith
1141 east palm street
<u>washington, la 98654</u>

   Ⓐ Washington, LA 98654
   Ⓑ Washington, La 98654
   Ⓒ washington, LA 98654
   Ⓓ washington, La 98654

8. Edit the below sentence for capitalization. Choose the sentence that is written correctly.

Next Semester, I plan to take English, History, Math, Spanish, and Music.

   Ⓐ Next Semester, I plan to take English, History, Spanish, and music.
   Ⓑ Next semester, I plan to take English, History, Spanish, and Music.
   Ⓒ Next semester, I plan to take english, history, spanish, and music.
   Ⓓ Next semester, I plan to take English, history, Spanish, and music.

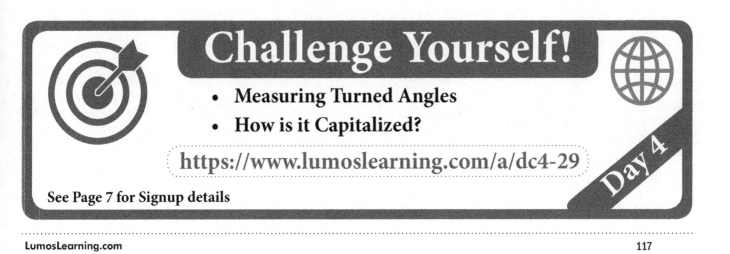

Challenge Yourself!

- **Measuring Turned Angles**
- **How is it Capitalized?**

https://www.lumoslearning.com/a/dc4-29

Day 4

See Page 7 for Signup details

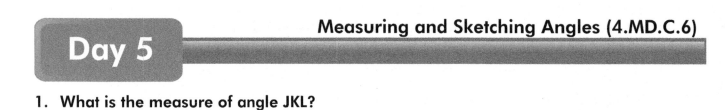

1. **What is the measure of angle JKL?**

Ⓐ 65 degrees
Ⓑ 115 degrees
Ⓒ 75 degrees
Ⓓ 140 degrees

2. **What is the measure of this angle?**

Ⓐ 10 degrees
Ⓑ 28 degrees
Ⓒ 48 degrees
Ⓓ 90 degrees

3. **What is the measure of angle PQR?**

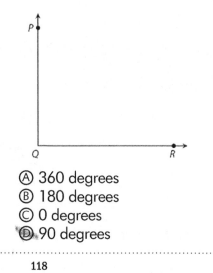

Ⓐ 360 degrees
Ⓑ 180 degrees
Ⓒ 0 degrees
Ⓓ 90 degrees

4. Which angle is equal to $\frac{1}{6}$ of a whole turn?
Shade the figure below to represent the answer.
Instruction: 1 shaded cell = 10 degrees.

What's the Punctuation? (L.4.2.B/C)

Day 5

5. Choose the sentence that is punctuated correctly. Circle the correct answer choice.

Ⓐ Before I go to bed each night I brush my teeth.
Ⓑ The rabbit scampered across the yard, and ran into the woods.
Ⓒ I don't like to watch scary movies but I like to read scary books.
Ⓓ Our teacher gave us time to study before she gave us the test.

6. Choose the sentence that correctly punctuates a quotation. Circle the correct answer choice.

Ⓐ "Did you remember to lock the door," asked Jenny?
Ⓑ "Did you remember to lock the door? asked Jenny."
Ⓒ Jenny asked "Did you remember to lock the door?"
Ⓓ Jenny asked, "Did you remember to lock the door?"

7. Choose the sentence that contains a punctuation error.

Ⓐ Cindy wants to go to the mall this afternoon, but her mother will not let her.
Ⓑ Wendy stayed up all night completing her science project, but forgot to take it with her.
Ⓒ Henry forgot to close the gate securely, so his dog escaped from the backyard.
Ⓓ Jimmy and John joined the Army; Billy and George joined the Navy.

8. What is the correct way to write the sentence below?

Do you know Shel Silverstein's poem The Boa Constrictor our teacher asked.

Ⓐ "Do you know Shel Silverstein's poem 'The Boa Constrictor'?" our teacher asked.
Ⓑ "Do you know Shel Silverstein's poem "The Boa Constrictor"? our teacher asked.
Ⓒ "Do you know Shel Silverstein's poem The Boa Constrictor"? our teacher asked.
Ⓓ "Do you know Shel Silverstein's poem The Boa Constrictor" she asked?

Challenge Yourself!
• Measuring and Sketching Angles
• What's the Punctuation?

https://www.lumoslearning.com/a/dc4-30

Day 5

See Page 7 for Signup details

This Week's Online Activities

- **Reading Assignment**
- **Vocabulary Practice**
- **Write Your Summer Diary**

https://www.lumoslearning.com/a/slh4-5

See Page 7 for Signup details

Weekly Fun Summer Photo Contest

Take a picture of your summer fun activity and share it on Twitter or Instagram

Use the **#SummerLearning** mention

@LumosLearning on Twitter or

@lumos.learning on Instagram

Tag friends and increase your chances of winning the contest

Participate and stand a chance to WIN $50 Amazon gift card!

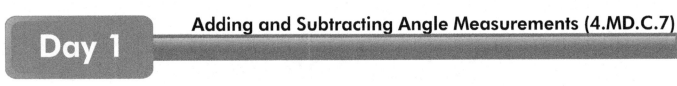

1. Angle 1 measures 40 degrees, and angle 2 measures 30 degrees. What is the measure of angle of PQR?

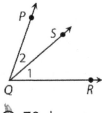

Ⓐ 70 degrees
Ⓑ 80 degrees
Ⓒ 100 degrees
Ⓓ 10 degrees

2. Angle ADC measures 120 degrees, and angle ADB measures 95 degrees. What is the measure of angle BDC?

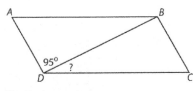

Ⓐ 5 degrees
Ⓑ 35 degrees
Ⓒ 15 degrees
Ⓓ 25 degrees

3. Angle JNM measures 100 degrees, angle JNK measures 25 degree, and angle KNL measures 35 degrees. What is the measure of angle LNM?

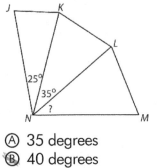

Ⓐ 35 degrees
Ⓑ 40 degrees
Ⓒ 30 degrees
Ⓓ 25 degrees

4. What is the value of x° and y° in the figure below. Circle the correct answer

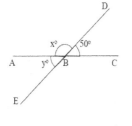

- Ⓐ x° = 120° and y° = 60°
- Ⓑ x° = 130° and y° = 50°
- Ⓒ x° = 50° and y° = 130°
- Ⓓ x° = 110° and y° = 70°

How is it Spelled? (L.4.2.D)

Day 1

5. Choose the correctly spelled work that best completes the sentence.

Vargas asked his partner, "Could you please _____ your question to make it easier to understand?"

- Ⓐ clearify
- Ⓑ Clerify
- Ⓒ carefully
- Ⓓ clarify

6. Find the misspelled word.

- Ⓐ ostrich
- Ⓑ vehicel
- Ⓒ wings
- Ⓓ horse

7. Which of the following words are spelled correctly?

- Ⓐ pollution
- Ⓑ polution
- Ⓒ plloution
- Ⓓ polltion

8. ____ v ____ n ____ ____

Fill in the missing vowels to make a proper word.

Ⓐ ivinae
Ⓑ avinie
Ⓒ avenue
Ⓓ evenie

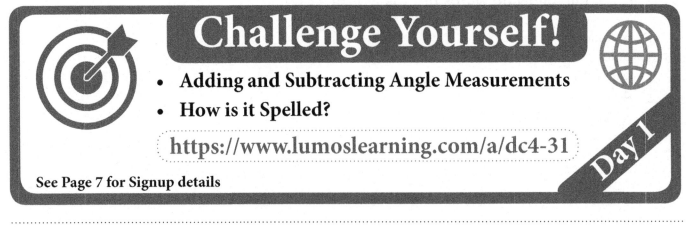

Day 2

1. Which of the following is a quadrilateral?

Ⓐ Triangle
Ⓑ Rhombus
Ⓒ Pentagon
Ⓓ Hexagon

2. How many sides does a pentagon have?

Ⓐ 3
Ⓑ 2
Ⓒ 1
Ⓓ 5

3. Use the network below to respond to the following question: How many line segments connect directly to Vertex F?

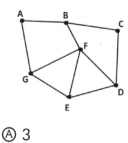

Ⓐ 3
Ⓑ 4
Ⓒ 5
Ⓓ 6

4. With reference to the figure below, which of the following statements are correct? Select all the correct answers.

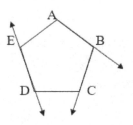

Ⓐ There are 2 rays.
Ⓑ There are 3 line segments.
Ⓒ There is one line.
Ⓓ There is no line.

5. Choose the word that best completes the sentence.
Alexander _____ into the living room to show off his new suit. He had a very high opinion of himself!

Ⓐ walked
Ⓑ strutted
Ⓒ trudged
Ⓓ waddled

6. Choose the word that best completes the sentence.
Collecting the garbage was _____ work, but Tom was happy to do it. The job wore on his body, especially during the hottest days of summer, but he knew he was providing an important public service to his community.

Ⓐ uncomfortable
Ⓑ grueling
Ⓒ bad
Ⓓ stupid

7. Choose the word that best completes sentence.
Dante was _____ about his award for most improved swimmer. He had never wanted anything more!

Ⓐ peaceful
Ⓑ happy
Ⓒ elated
Ⓓ disappointed

8. Choose the word that best completes the sentence.
The baby babbled sweetly, making it difficult for her mother to be upset about the _____ mess she had made when she threw spaghetti all over the kitchen.

Ⓐ gigantic
Ⓑ big
Ⓒ wide
Ⓓ deep

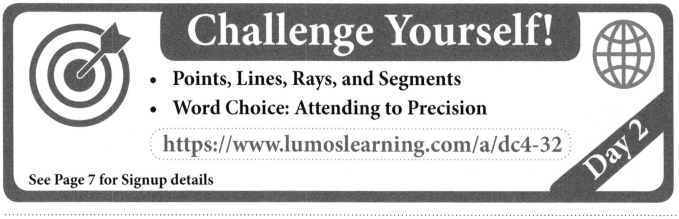

Challenge Yourself!

• **Points, Lines, Rays, and Segments**
• **Word Choice: Attending to Precision**

https://www.lumoslearning.com/a/dc4-32

Day 2

See Page 7 for Signup details

Day 3

1. The hands of this clock form a(n) _____ angle.

    Ⓐ obtuse
    Ⓑ straight
    Ⓒ right
    Ⓓ acute

2. How many acute angles and obtuse angles are there in the figure shown below?

    Ⓐ 2 acute angles and 6 obtuse angles
    Ⓑ 4 acute angles and 4 obtuse angles
    Ⓒ 8 acute angles and 0 obtuse angles
    Ⓓ 0 acute angles and 8 obtuse angles

3. Describe the angles found in this figure.

    Ⓐ 2 right angles and 3 acute angles
    Ⓑ 3 right angles and 2 obtuse angles
    Ⓒ 2 right angles, 2 obtuse angles, and 1 acute angle
    Ⓓ 2 right angles and 3 obtuse angles

4. Choose the letters among the following which have at least one right angle. Note that there may be more than one correct answer.

    Ⓐ L
    Ⓑ T
    Ⓒ V
    Ⓓ E

5. Choose the punctuation that means Jermain's mother is speaking to him.
Jermaine mother said you have to clean your room.

Ⓐ Jermaine mother said you have to clean your room.
Ⓑ "Jermaine, Mother said you have to clean your room."
Ⓒ Jermaine Mother said, "You have to clean your room."
Ⓓ "Jermaine," Mother said, "you have to clean your room."

6. Choose the punctuation that means a third character is shouting at Jermaine to tell him his mother said to clean his room.
Jermaine mother said you have to clean your room.

Ⓐ "Jermaine," Mother said, "you have to clean your room!"
Ⓑ "Jermaine, Mother said you have to clean your room!"
Ⓒ "Jermaine," Mother said, "you have to clean your room?"
Ⓓ "Jermaine, Mother said you have to clean your room."

7. Choose the most appropriate end punctuation.
Dante was elated about his award for most improved swimmer. He had never wanted anything more

Ⓐ .
Ⓑ ?
Ⓒ !
Ⓓ $

8. Choose the sentence that is punctuated correctly.

Ⓐ The tiger crept carefully through the jungle?
Ⓑ The tiger crept carefully through the jungle!
Ⓒ The tiger crept carefully through the jungle
Ⓓ The tiger crept carefully through the jungle.

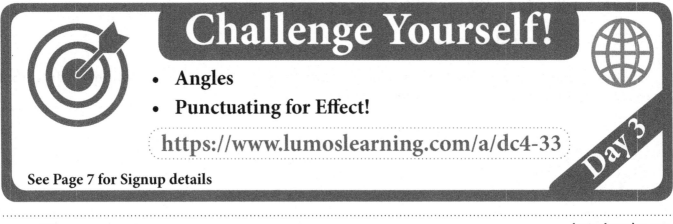

Challenge Yourself!

- **Angles**
- **Punctuating for Effect!**

https://www.lumoslearning.com/a/dc4-33

Day 3

See Page 7 for Signup details

1. **Complete the sentence:**
   A polygon is named based on _____.

   Ⓐ how many sides or interior angles it has
   Ⓑ how many of its sides are straight
   Ⓒ how large it is
   Ⓓ how many lines of symmetry it has

2. **Complete the sentence:**
   A polygon with 4 sides and 4 interior angles is called a(n) _____.

   Ⓐ triangle
   Ⓑ quadrilateral
   Ⓒ pentagon
   Ⓓ octagon

3. **Complete the sentence:**
   A rectangle must have _____ .

   Ⓐ All parallel sides and all congruent sides
   Ⓑ 2 pairs of parallel sides and 2 pairs of congruent sides
   Ⓒ 2 pairs of parallel sides and 4 congruent sides
   Ⓓ 4 parallel sides and 2 pairs of congruent sides

4. **For each statement given in the first column, select true, if it is correct or select false, if it is wrong.**

	True	False
An acute triangle can be an equilateral triangle	Ⓧ	○
An acute triangle cannot be an isosceles triangle	○	Ⓧ
An acute triangle cannot be a scalene triangle	○	Ⓧ
All right triangles are scalene triangles	○	Ⓧ
An obtuse triangle can be an isosceles triangle	Ⓧ	○
An obtuse triangle can be a scalene triangle	Ⓧ	○

5. **What does the word *extracted* mean in the below sentence?**
The milk is extracted from the coconut, which is used to prepare a variety of dishes and sweets.

Ⓐ To put in
Ⓑ To take out of something
Ⓒ To make
Ⓓ To throw out

6. **Using context clues from the below sentence, the word *despondent* means: Circle the correct answer choice.**
The poor woman was despondent after losing everything she owned in the fire.

Ⓐ excited
Ⓑ questioning
Ⓒ disheartened
Ⓓ radiant

7. **Based on the below sentence, console means: Circle the correct answer choice.**
My father tried to <u>console</u> me after my dog died, but nothing he did made me feel better.

Ⓐ entertain
Ⓑ comfort
Ⓒ talk to
Ⓓ explain

8. The sleepy kittens crawled into bed with their mother. They quickly nestled cozily beside her and went to sleep.

The word *nestled* means:

Ⓐ purred softly
Ⓑ lay down
Ⓒ leaned against
Ⓓ snuggled up to

Challenge Yourself!

- **Classifying Plane (2-D) Shapes**
- **Finding the Meaning**

https://www.lumoslearning.com/a/dc4-34

Day 4

See Page 7 for Signup details

Day 5

1. **How many lines of symmetry does an equilateral triangle have?**

   Ⓐ 1
   Ⓑ 3
   Ⓒ 2
   Ⓓ 0

2. **How many lines of symmetry does a regular pentagon have?**

   Ⓐ 1
   Ⓑ 2
   Ⓒ 5
   Ⓓ 10

3. **How many lines of symmetry does a rectangle have?**

   Ⓐ 1
   Ⓑ 2
   Ⓒ 3
   Ⓓ 4

4. **Select the heart with the correct line of symmetry below by circling it.**

5. What is the meaning of the word, "sentiment," in the paragraph below?

Franklin D. Roosevelt gave his first inaugural address in 1933, during the midst of the Great Depression. He famously said, "The only thing we have to fear is… fear itself." His <u>sentiment</u> helped assuage the fears of many Americans, giving them hope for better days ahead.

Ⓐ a person who often cries
Ⓑ a view or attitude toward a situation or event
Ⓒ a nice piece of jewelry
Ⓓ blame

6. What is the meaning of the word, "assuage," in the paragraph below?

Franklin D. Roosevelt gave his first inaugural address in 1933, during the midst of the Great Depression. He famously said, "The only thing we have to fear is… fear itself." This sentiment helped <u>assuage</u> the fears of many Americans, giving them hope for better days ahead.

Ⓐ to make worse
Ⓑ to ease
Ⓒ to heighten
Ⓓ to strengthen

7. What is the meaning of the word, "affluent," in the paragraph below?

The restaurant catered to an <u>affluent</u> crowd. The food was very expensive, the tablecloths were crisp and white, and patrons were expected to dress nicely.

Ⓐ practical
Ⓑ wealthy
Ⓒ honest
Ⓓ poor

8. What is the meaning of the word, "patrons," in the paragraph below?

The restaurant catered to an affluent crowd. The food was very expensive, the tablecloths were crisp and white, and <u>patrons</u> were expected to dress nicely in order to eat there.

- Ⓐ doctors
- Ⓑ waiters
- Ⓒ cooks
- Ⓓ customers

Challenge Yourself!

- Symmetry
- Context Clues

https://www.lumoslearning.com/a/dc4-35

Day 5

See Page 7 for Signup details

Cross Word Puzzles

DOWN

ACROSS

DOWN: 1. Wisp 2. Shaver 3. Toothpaste 4. Hairdryer 5. Hairbrush 6. Shampoo 7. Bathrobe
ACROSS: 6. Spray 8. Brush 9. Mirror 10. Soap 11. Toothbrush 12. Towel

1. Grandpiano 2. Xylophone 3. Harp 4. Accordion 5.(across) Castanets 5. (down) Cello 6. Violin 7. Cymbals
8. Synthesizer 9. Triangle 10. Guitar 11. Trumpet 12. Melodica 13. Drum 14. Tambourine 15. Saxophone 16. Maracas

This Week's Online Activities

- **Reading Assignment**
- **Vocabulary Practice**
- **Write Your Summer Diary**

https://www.lumoslearning.com/a/slh4-5

See Page 7 for Signup details

Weekly Fun Summer Photo Contest

Take a picture of your summer fun activity and share it on Twitter or Instagram

Use the **#SummerLearning** mention

@LumosLearning on Twitter or

@lumos.learning on Instagram

Tag friends and increase your chances of winning the contest

Participate and stand a chance to WIN $50 Amazon gift card!

Week 8 Summer Practice

1. Cindy's mother baked cookies for the school bake sale. Monday she baked 4 dozen cookies. Tuesday she baked 3 dozen cookies. Wednesday she baked 4 dozen cookies. After she finished baking Thursday afternoon, she took 15 dozen cookies to the bake sale. Which equation shows how to determine the amount of cookies that she baked on Thursday?

Ⓐ 4 + 3 + 4 + n = 15
Ⓑ 4 + 3 + 4 = n
Ⓒ 4 x 3 x 4 x n = 15
Ⓓ 15 ÷ 11 = n

2. There are 9 students in Mrs. Whitten's class. She gave each student the same number of Popsicle sticks. There were 47 Popsicle sticks in her bag. To decide how many sticks each student received, Larry wrote the following number sentence: 47 ÷ 9 = n. How many Popsicle sticks were left in the bag after dividing them evenly among the 9 students?

Ⓐ 0
Ⓑ 2
Ⓒ 3
Ⓓ 4

3. Sixty-three students visited the science exhibit. The remainder of the visitors were adults. One hundred forty-seven people visited the science exhibit in all.
How would you determine how many of the visitors were adults?

Ⓐ 63 + 147 = n
Ⓑ 147 ÷ 63 = n
Ⓒ 147 ÷ n = 63
Ⓓ 63 + n = 147

4. Create an equation from the following situation: Tim had a box of chocolates. He started with 18 chocolates, but then gave 6 to his friends. How many does he have left?

5. Mindy was surprised to discover how disorganized the students had left the books. What is the meaning of the word <u>disorganized</u>?

Ⓐ organized
Ⓑ not organized
Ⓒ neat
Ⓓ torn

6. Which of the following words contains a prefix that means <u>again</u>?

Ⓐ preview
Ⓑ international
Ⓒ rewind
Ⓓ disagree

7. Which of the following words refers to half of the globe?

Ⓐ longitude
Ⓑ hemisphere
Ⓒ parallel
Ⓓ latitude

8. In the word 'bewailed', the prefix is _____.

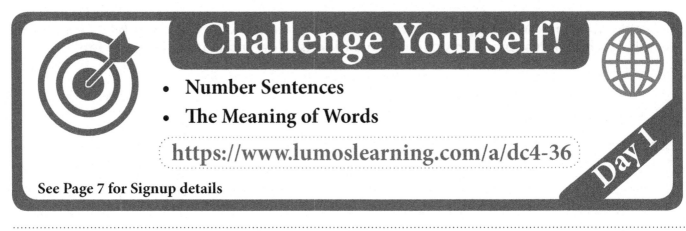

Challenge Yourself!

- **Number Sentences**
- **The Meaning of Words**

https://www.lumoslearning.com/a/dc4-36

See Page 7 for Signup details

Day 1

Day 2

1. **Markers are sold in packs of 18 and 24. Yolanda bought five of the smaller packs and ten of the larger packs. How many markers did she buy altogether?**

   Ⓐ 42 markers
   Ⓑ 432 markers
   Ⓒ 320 markers
   Ⓓ 330 markers

2. **Each box of cookies contains 48 cookies. About how many cookies would be in 18 boxes?**

   Ⓐ 100 cookies
   Ⓑ 500 cookies
   Ⓒ 1,000 cookies
   Ⓓ 2,000 cookies

3. **At RTA Elementary School, there are 16 more female teachers than male teachers. If there are 60 female teachers, how can you find the number of male teachers in the school?**

   Ⓐ Subtract 16 from 60
   Ⓑ Multiply 16 by 60
   Ⓒ Add 16 to 60
   Ⓓ Divide 60 by 16

4. **Luke has two bags of pennies. The first bag has 8 and the second bag has 6 times as many pennies as the first bag. How many pennies are in the second bag? Match each number to the correct name by darkening the circle.**

	Multiplier	Number in original set	Number in second bag
48	○	○	○
8	○	○	○
6	○	○	○

5. **Where would one look to find the definition of a key word when reading a science textbook?**

Ⓐ the glossary
Ⓑ the thesaurus
Ⓒ the dictionary
Ⓓ the table of contents

6. **What part of speech is the word, "component," in the thesaurus entry below?**

Component. — n. component; component part, integral part, integrant part; element, constituent, ingredient, leaven; part and parcel; contents; appurtenance; feature

Ⓐ adjective
Ⓑ verb
Ⓒ adverb
Ⓓ noun

7. **According to the thesaurus entry below, what is a synonym for the word, "veteran?"**

Veteran.— n. veteran, old man, seer, patriarch, graybeard; grandfather, grandsire; grandam; gaffer, gammer; crone; pantaloon; sexagenarian, octogenarian, nonagenarian, centenarian; old stager.

Ⓐ veterinarian
Ⓑ graybeard
Ⓒ young man
Ⓓ None of the above

8. Which of the following is NOT a synonym for "edge?"

Edge. — n. edge, verge, brink, brow, brim, margin, border, confine, skirt, rim, flange, side, mouth; jaws, chops, chaps, fauces; lip, muzzle. threshold, door, porch; portal &c. (opening) 260; coast, shore. frame, fringe, flounce, frill, list, trimming, edging, skirting, hem, selvedge, welt, furbelow, valance, gimp. adj. border, marginal, skirting; labial, labiated, marginated.

Ⓐ brink
Ⓑ flank
Ⓒ verge
Ⓓ rim

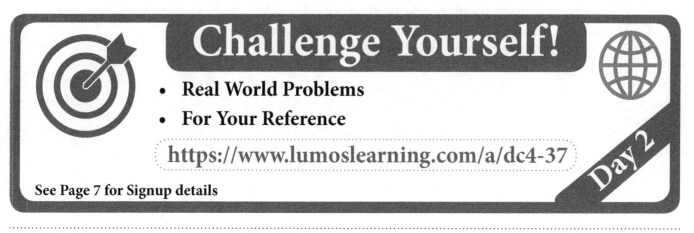

Day 3

1. Jam jars can be packed in large boxes of 60 or small boxes of 25. There are 700 jam jars to be shipped. The supplier wants to use the least number of boxes possible, but the boxes cannot be only partially filled. How many large boxes will the supplier end up using?

   Ⓐ 10 large boxes
   Ⓑ 11 large boxes
   Ⓒ 12 large boxes
   Ⓓ It is not possible to ship all 700 jars.

2. Allison needs 400 feet of rope to put a border around her yard. She can buy the rope in lengths of 36 feet. How many 36 foot long ropes will she need to buy?

   Ⓐ 9 ropes
   Ⓑ 10 ropes
   Ⓒ 11 ropes
   Ⓓ 12 ropes.

3. Katie and her friend went to the county fair. They each brought a $20.00 bill. The admission fee was $4.00 per person. Ride tickets cost 50 cents each. If each ride required two tickets per person, how many rides was each girl able to go on?

   Ⓐ 16 rides
   Ⓑ 32 rides
   Ⓒ 8 rides
   Ⓓ 20 rides

4. George and Michael are both in fourth grade, but attend different schools. George goes to Hillside Elementary and Michael goes to Sunnyside Elementary. Hillside has 7 fourth grade classes with 18 students in each class. Sunnyside has 5 fourth grade classes with 21 students in each class. Mark which of the following are correct responses.

   Ⓐ Hillside has 126 fourth grade students.
   Ⓑ Sunnyside has 100 fourth grade students.
   Ⓒ Sunnyside has fewer fourth grade students than Hillside.
   Ⓓ There are 21 more students at Hillside than Sunnyside.
   Ⓔ There are 26 more students at Hillside than Sunnyside.

5. What does the metaphor in the first sentence mean?

The sky was an angry, purple monster. It roared fiercely as the thunder crashed and the rain poured down.

    Ⓐ The sky had clouds in the shape of a monster.
    Ⓑ The sky was stormy.
    Ⓒ Monsters invaded the town.
    Ⓓ None of the above

6. What purpose does the author's simile serve in the paragraph?

In the days after Dad was laid off almost everyone was gloomy. Sam didn't smile, <u>Mom hovered over everyone like a cloud full of rain</u>. It was Sasha who was the ray of sunshine when she declared, "It's alright. Hugs are free!"

    Ⓐ It describes the setting after Dad was laid off.
    Ⓑ It makes the point that mom was gloomy and likely to cry.
    Ⓒ It shows that Sasha was a happy, upbeat presence in the house.
    Ⓓ It reminds us that hugs are free.

7. By comparing Kevin to a brick wall, what is the speaker trying to say about Kevin?

The starting goalie was out with an injury, so Kevin was finally getting his chance to prove his worth. He knew he could do it. He was ready. Kevin was a brick wall.

    Ⓐ He would not allow the opponent to score he'd block the goal posts.
    Ⓑ He was hard-headed.
    Ⓒ He built a wall in front of his soccer goal.
    Ⓓ He threw bricks at his opponent.

8. What purpose does the author's metaphor serve in the paragraph?

In the days after Dad was laid off almost everyone was gloomy. Sam didn't smile, Mom hovered over everyone like a cloud full of rain. <u>It was Sasha who was the ray of sunshine when she declared, "It's alright. Hugs are free!"</u>

   Ⓐ It describes the setting after Dad was laid off.
   Ⓑ It makes the point that mom was gloomy and likely to cry.
   Ⓒ It shows that Sasha was a happy, upbeat presence in the house.
   Ⓓ It reminds us that hugs are free.

Challenge Yourself!

- **Multi-Step Problems**
- **Similes and Metaphors**

https://www.lumoslearning.com/a/dc4-38

Day 3

See Page 7 for Signup details

Day 4

1. **Which number can be divided evenly into 28?**

   Ⓐ 3
   Ⓑ 6
   Ⓒ 7
   Ⓓ 5

2. **Use the Venn diagram below to respond to the following question.**
   Which of the following numbers would be found in Region D?

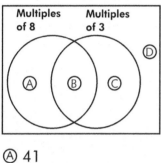

   Ⓐ 41
   Ⓑ 53
   Ⓒ 62
   Ⓓ All of the above

3. **Which of these sets contains no composite numbers?**

   Ⓐ 97, 71, 59, 29
   Ⓑ 256, 155, 75, 15
   Ⓒ 5, 23, 87, 91
   Ⓓ 2, 11, 19, 51

4. **Identify the prime number and write it in the box given below:**

   13,15,9,100,28,77

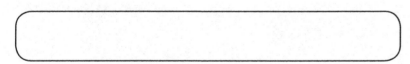

5. What is meant by the idiom _hit the ceiling_ in the below sentence?

If Wendy's dad found out that she took her cell phone to school, he would hit the ceiling.

Ⓐ Wendy's dad will jump high.
Ⓑ Wendy's dad will be very angry.
Ⓒ Wendy's dad will laugh loudly.
Ⓓ Wendy's dad will congratulate her.

6. What is meant by the idiom swallow your pride?

I think that you need to swallow your pride and apologize to your teacher for talking in class.

Ⓐ to swallow hard
Ⓑ to deny doing something
Ⓒ to forget about being embarrassed
Ⓓ to pretend you are sorry

7. What does the idiom 'walking on air' mean?

Mindy was walking on air after she went backstage and met Adam Levine.

Ⓐ Mindy was floating through the air.
Ⓑ Mindy was dreaming.
Ⓒ Mindy was in a state of bliss.
Ⓓ Mindy was disappointed.

8. Which sentence contains an idiom? Circle the correct answer choice.

Ⓐ It's raining cats and dogs outside!
Ⓑ It's thundering loudly outside.
Ⓒ It rained 6 inches last week.
Ⓓ Wear a raincoat and boots, because it's raining really hard outside.

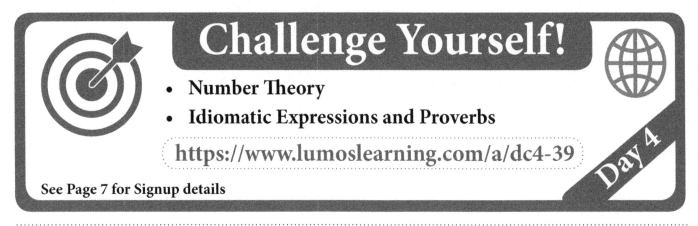

Challenge Yourself!

- **Number Theory**
- **Idiomatic Expressions and Proverbs**

https://www.lumoslearning.com/a/dc4-39

See Page 7 for Signup details

Day 4

Day 5

1. **What is the missing number in this pattern?**
   24, 36, ___, 60, 72

   Ⓐ 50
   Ⓑ 54
   Ⓒ 48
   Ⓓ 46

2. **Study the following pattern. Then find the next two terms.**
   0, 10, 8, 18, 16, 26, 24, ___, ___

   Ⓐ 36, 34
   Ⓑ 34, 44
   Ⓒ 32, 30
   Ⓓ 34, 32

3. **Darren was skip-counting by 5's starting from 2. He said, "2, 7, 12, 17, . . ." After a while, he noticed a pattern in the numbers. Based on the pattern, which of the following numbers will Darren eventually say?**

   Ⓐ 720
   Ⓑ 275
   Ⓒ 187
   Ⓓ 271

4. **Fill in the missing boxes in the table to complete each pattern or sequence of numbers start from the left side of the table to complete the sequence.**

1		3	4		6
2	4		8	10	
	12	18		30	36
10		18	22	26	

Day 5

5. Choose the correct set of synonyms for "*small.*"

- Ⓐ enormous, giant
- Ⓑ minute, gargantuan
- Ⓒ small, unseen
- Ⓓ miniature, minute

6. Choose the correct set of *synonyms*.

- Ⓐ unrealistic, believable
- Ⓑ noteworthy, important
- Ⓒ noteworthy, insignificant
- Ⓓ unfair, just

7. Choose the correct set of *antonyms*.

- Ⓐ radiant, dull
- Ⓑ rescue, save
- Ⓒ chortle, laugh
- Ⓓ sparkle, shine

8. Pick the Synonyms for the word Peek from the list below and write it in the box given below.
Stare, Glance, Ogle, glimpse, look, watch

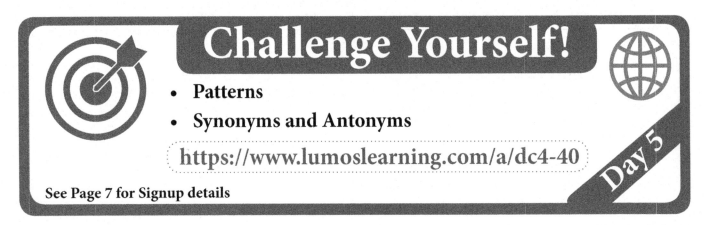

Challenge Yourself!

- **Patterns**
- **Synonyms and Antonyms**

https://www.lumoslearning.com/a/dc4-40

See Page 7 for Signup details

Day 5

This Week's Online Activities

- **Reading Assignment**
- **Vocabulary Practice**
- **Write Your Summer Diary**

https://www.lumoslearning.com/a/slh4-5

See Page 7 for Signup details

Weekly Fun Summer Photo Contest

Take a picture of your summer fun activity and share it on Twitter or Instagram

Use the **#SummerLearning** mention

@LumosLearning on Twitter or

@lumos.learning on Instagram

Tag friends and increase your chances of winning the contest

Participate and stand a chance to WIN $50 Amazon gift card!

1. Which number is in the thousands place in the number 984,923?

   Ⓐ 9
   Ⓑ 8
   Ⓒ 4
   Ⓓ 2

2. What is the value of the 8 in 683,345?

   Ⓐ 80
   Ⓑ 800
   Ⓒ 8,000
   Ⓓ 80,000

3. Which number equals 4 thousands, 6 hundreds, 0 tens, and 5 ones?

   Ⓐ 465
   Ⓑ 4,605
   Ⓒ 4,650
   Ⓓ 4,065

4. John has $500. Karen has 10 times as much money. How much money does Karen have? Write your answer in the box below

   ⟨   ⟩

5. Choose the word that best completes the sentence.

When Jeremy arrived home his mom _____ him about the dance until he could think of no more details to give her.

Ⓐ yelled at
Ⓑ quizzed
Ⓒ praised
Ⓓ waddled

6. Choose the word that best completes the sentence.

The woodlands of the midatlantic region are filled with all sorts of interesting _____.

Ⓐ movies
Ⓑ wildlife
Ⓒ colleges
Ⓓ mortar

7. Choose the word that best completes sentence.

The _____ John Muir helped preserve our country's natural beauty by helping to establish Yosemite National Park.

Ⓐ antagoinist
Ⓑ pianist
Ⓒ conservationist
Ⓓ statistician

8. Choose the word that best completes the sentence.

Sarah was _____ at the news that the giant oak she had worked to protect was going to be removed in order to build a parking lot.

Ⓐ crestfallen
Ⓑ starstruck
Ⓒ jovial
Ⓓ greedy

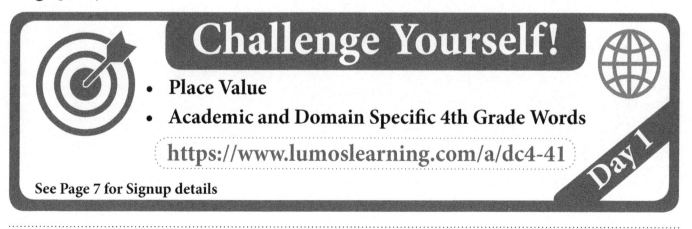

Challenge Yourself!

- **Place Value**
- **Academic and Domain Specific 4th Grade Words**

https://www.lumoslearning.com/a/dc4-41

Day 1

See Page 7 for Signup details

Day 2

1. **Which statement is NOT true?**

   Ⓐ 798 < 799
   Ⓑ 798 > 789
   Ⓒ 798 < 789
   Ⓓ 798 = 798

2. **Write the expanded form of this number.**
   954,351

   Ⓐ 90,000 + 5,000 + 400 + 30 + 5 + 1
   Ⓑ 900,000 + 50,000 + 4,000 + 300 + 50 + 1
   Ⓒ 900,000 + 54,000 + 300 + 50 + 1
   Ⓓ 900,000 + 50,000 + 4,000 + 300 + 51

3. **What is the standard form of this number?**
   30,000 + 200 + 50

   Ⓐ 30,250
   Ⓑ 32,500
   Ⓒ 325,000
   Ⓓ 3,250

4. **Write the expanded form of the number shown below in the given box with a comma in the correct place.**

   2,000 + 500 + 9

(1) Mary went to visit her grandmother last weekend. (2) She likes to visit her grandmother frequently. (3) While visiting, they enjoy walking. (4) They strolled in the beautiful park and talked. (5) Mary and her grandmother enjoyed their visit.

5. Which sentences contain a conjunction?

Ⓐ   sentences 1 and 2
Ⓑ   sentences 2 and 3
Ⓒ   sentences 3 and 4
Ⓓ   sentences 4 and 5

6. Billy does not like to play basketball, nor does he enjoy watching it on TV. Identify the conjunction in the above sentence.

Ⓐ   not
Ⓑ   nor
Ⓒ   does
Ⓓ   to

7. As soon as I finish my homework, I am going to watch my favorite TV show. Identify the subordinating conjunction in the above sentence.

Ⓐ   soon
Ⓑ   as soon as
Ⓒ   to
Ⓓ   to watch

8. Go put on either your shoes and your boots. Fix the sentence by replacing and with an appropriate conjunction.

Challenge Yourself!

- **Compare Numbers and Expanded Notation**
- **Conjunctions and Interjections**

https://www.lumoslearning.com/a/dc4-42

Day 2

See Page 7 for Signup details

Day 3

1. **Round 4,170,154 to the nearest hundred thousand.**

   Ⓐ 4,200,000
   Ⓑ 4,180,000
   Ⓒ 4,179,000
   Ⓓ 4,100,000

2. **Round 4,170,154 to the nearest million.**

   Ⓐ 4,000,000
   Ⓑ 4,180,000
   Ⓒ 4,179,000
   Ⓓ 5,000,000

3. **Round 424,819 to the nearest ten.**

   Ⓐ 400,820
   Ⓑ 424,810
   Ⓒ 424,020
   Ⓓ 424,820

4. **Match each statement with the way in which it is rounded.**

	Nearest 10	Nearest 100	Nearest 1,000	Nearest 10,000
4,893 rounded to 4,890	○	○	○	○
15,309 rounded to 20,000	○	○	○	○
32,350 rounded to 32,000	○	○	○	○
523 rounded to 500	○	○	○	○

5. "I picked it up on the beach last weekend."
   In the above sentence, find the simple predicate.

   Ⓐ picked it up
   Ⓑ I
   Ⓒ I picked it
   Ⓓ picked

6. Choose the correct word to fill in the blank.
   I heard a sound. Did you _____ a sound?

   Ⓐ hearing
   Ⓑ heard
   Ⓒ hear
   Ⓓ will hear

7. Mary sang in the school choir last year, but this year she _____ in the church choir.
   Choose the correct verb for the above sentence.

   Ⓐ sung
   Ⓑ had sang
   Ⓒ is singing
   Ⓓ has sung

8. This morning I cleaned my room.

   Identify the simple predicate in the sentence above. Circle the correct answer choice.

   Ⓐ This
   Ⓑ morning
   Ⓒ cleaned
   Ⓓ room

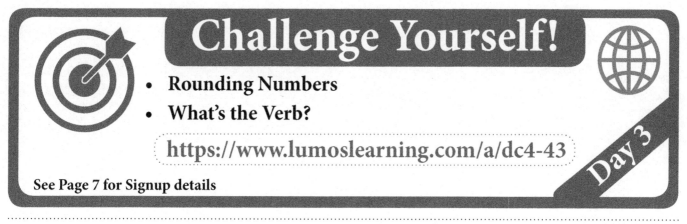

Challenge Yourself!

- **Rounding Numbers**
- **What's the Verb?**

https://www.lumoslearning.com/a/dc4-43

Day 3

See Page 7 for Signup details

Day 4

1. **Find the sum.**
   24 + 37 + 76 + 13

   Ⓐ 140
   Ⓑ 150
   Ⓒ 151
   Ⓓ None of these

2. **Find the difference.**
   702 - 314 = _____

   Ⓐ 388
   Ⓑ 412
   Ⓒ 312
   Ⓓ 402

3. **What is the sum of 0.55 + 6.35?**

   Ⓐ 6.09
   Ⓑ 11 0.85
   Ⓒ 6.90
   Ⓓ None of these

4. **Select all of the following expressions that will equal 4,189.**

   Ⓐ 4,002 + 187
   Ⓑ 6,100 − 2,189
   Ⓒ 12,555 − 8,366
   Ⓓ 859 + 3,985

5. (1) Kelly and her sister picked strawberries today. (2) When they arrived home, they decided to make strawberry jam.
   Choose the meaning of the word jam in sentence 2.

   Ⓐ to pack tightly
   Ⓑ a fruit spread like jelly
   Ⓒ become stuck
   Ⓓ an informal gathering of musicians

6. (1) I cannot stand to waste my time waiting in line. (2) It hurts my back to stand for so long.
   In sentence 1, the word stand means:

   Ⓐ tolerate or endure
   Ⓑ to undergo
   Ⓒ a small rack or table
   Ⓓ to maintain an upright position on your feet

7. (1) I cannot stand to waste my time waiting in line. (2) It hurts my back to stand for so long.
   In sentence 2, the word stand means:

   Ⓐ tolerate or endure
   Ⓑ to undergo
   Ⓒ a small rack or table
   Ⓓ to maintain an upright position on your feet

8. My mother went to the bank to deposit her pay check.
   Choose the sentence that uses the word bank in the same way. Circle the correct answer choice.

   Ⓐ My dad drove to the bank and withdrew some cash.
   Ⓑ We went fishing at the bank of the river.
   Ⓒ I can bank my passing grades and retake the tests I didn't pass.
   Ⓓ I am always right, and you can bank on that!

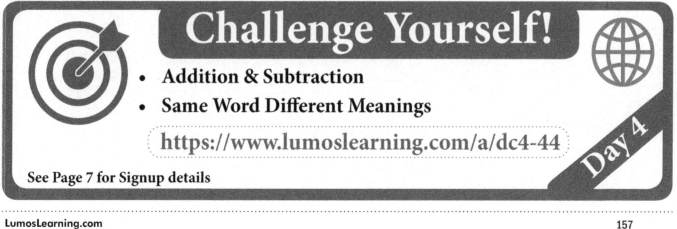

Challenge Yourself!

- **Addition & Subtraction**
- **Same Word Different Meanings**

https://www.lumoslearning.com/a/dc4-44

Day 4

See Page 7 for Signup details

Day 5

1. Which of the following number sentences illustrates the Associative Property of Multiplication?

   Ⓐ $4 \times 0 = 0$
   Ⓑ $77 \times 1 = 1 \times 77$
   Ⓒ $(2 \times 4) \times 5 = 2 \times (4 \times 5)$
   Ⓓ $13 \times 7 = (10 \times 7) + (3 \times 7)$

2. Solve.
   $4 \times 3 \times 6 =$ _____

   Ⓐ 48
   Ⓑ 72
   Ⓒ 56
   Ⓓ 64

3. Find the exact product of $5 \times 20 \times 8$.

   Ⓐ 800
   Ⓑ 560
   Ⓒ 80
   Ⓓ 900

4. Fill in the correct numbers to complete each multiplication sentence.

5	x		=	65
23	x	14	=	
	x	34	=	340
52	x		=	104

5. (The below passage uses which style of narration?

You didn't want to ask for a loan, but you had no choice. You spent all of your allowance at the ball-game, and now you don't have the money to buy your mom a birthday present.

Ⓐ First person
Ⓑ Second person
Ⓒ Third person
Ⓓ Fourth person

6. The below passage uses which style of narration?

Max went for a bike ride in the park. While on the ride, he saw his best friend, Sammy. They decided to go to the movies instead of bike riding in the park. Max called his mom and asked if it would be alright to go to the movie with his friend. She said yes, so Max and Sammy jumped on their bikes and went to see The Emoji Movie.

Ⓐ First person
Ⓑ Second person
Ⓒ Third person
Ⓓ Fourth person

7. The below passage uses which style of narration?

I had been craving chocolate ice cream all day. Finally, school was over and I could get a huge chocolate ice cream cone. The line was long, but it was worth the wait. The first taste of my ice cream cone was delicious. Then, the worst thing imaginable happened. I bumped into the person behind me and dropped my ice cream cone and it fell on the floor.

Ⓐ First person
Ⓑ Second person
Ⓒ Third person
Ⓓ Fourth person

Celia Cruz

She was born in Havana, Cuba in 1925. She was told by her grandmother that she could sing before she could talk. Her grandmother used to laugh and tell the family that she practiced her singing at night. (She was thought to have cried most of the night.) Cruz' work in radio during the 1940's in Cuba led to her fame and she traveled throughout Latin America with a female band. She won her first award singing on an amateur hour TV show. Cruz sang a version of a tango song that was very popular in Cuba.

In the 1950's Celia Cruz joined the Sonora Mantancera as a lead female singer. Then she was able to go to the Tropicana, the best establishment for Cuban music. If you performed at the Tropicana, you had made it in the singing world of Cubans.

She then went to Mexico for a one year contract right before Fidel Castro took over Cuba. She and her band never returned. Cruz moved to New York in 1961. By this time she was a well- known Cuban singer and independent from her band. She became known as the "Salsa Queen" due to her style of music. During the 1990's she gained great popularity among the younger generations, as her music reappeared. Cruz has been honored by five Presidents of the United States. She died of brain cancer in 2003, but her music and legend continue to thrive throughout the world.

8. **If you were to be a musician such as Celia Cruz, what type of music would you perform, where and why? Write your answer in the box below.**

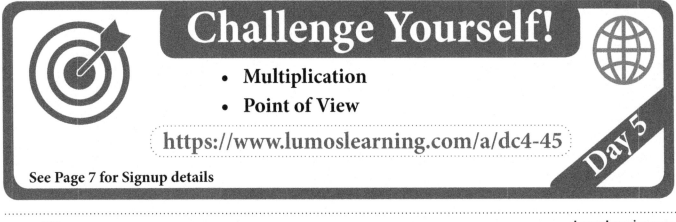

Challenge Yourself!

- Multiplication
- Point of View

https://www.lumoslearning.com/a/dc4-45

Day 5

See Page 7 for Signup details

This Week's Online Activities

- **Reading Assignment**
- **Vocabulary Practice**
- **Write Your Summer Diary**

https://www.lumoslearning.com/a/slh4-5

See Page 7 for Signup details

Weekly Fun Summer Photo Contest

Take a picture of your summer fun activity and share it on Twitter or Instagram

Use the **#SummerLearning** mention

@LumosLearning on Twitter or

@lumos.learning on Instagram

Tag friends and increase your chances of winning the contest

Participate and stand a chance to **WIN $50 Amazon gift card!**

Week 10

Lumos Short Story Competition 2022

Write a short story based on your summer experiences and get a chance to win $100 cash prize + 1 year free subscription to Lumos StepUp + trophy with a certificate.
To enter the competition follow the instructions.

Step 1

Visit **www.lumoslearning.com/a/tg4-5**
and register for online fun summer program.

Step 2

After registration, your child can upload their summer story by logging into the student portal and clicking on **Lumos Short Story Competition 2022.**

Note: *If you have already registered this book and using online resources need not register again. Students can simply log in to the student portal and submit their story for the competition.*
Visit: www.lumoslearning.com/a/slh2022 for more information

Last date for submission is August 31, 2022

Use the space provided below for scratch work before uploading your summer story Scratch Work

2021 Winning Story

In March 2020, I found out that my 7th-grade exams were canceled. At first, I was excited, but I soon realized that these changes would upend my expectations for school. Over time, my classmates and I realized that the global coronavirus pandemic was not something to be excited about and would have long-lasting effects on our education. My school canceled exams again this year, and, strangely, I found myself missing them. The virus has revealed global inequality regarding health.

Even as America fights the virus, so is it also fighting racism and injustice. The Black Lives Matter movement has shown me how brutal racism can be. The deaths of George Floyd and Breonna Taylor, two African Americans killed by police for no reason, have made me aware of the dangerous injustice in America. Hatred and violence against Asian immigrants are also on the rise. People of color in the US are routinely subjected to prejudice, if not also violence, at the hands of white people. Chinese people are blamed for the "China virus,"; which has led to Asian Americans being attacked. Enduring forms of racism are preventing progress around the world. Racism in society takes many forms, including prejudice, discrimination, and microaggressions. If racism is systemic in America, there will never be true peace or equality until it is uprooted. People see me as a person of color and assume that I'm from Africa because of the color of my skin, even though I am half Black and half white. I don't seem to earn as much respect as a white person would because I am thought of as a foreigner, not a true American. It makes me feel unwelcome and unwanted. I am lucky to have access to technology to keep me engaged in learning. There are still others who don't have the ability to continue learning, whose educational institutions have been shut down by the virus. I have learned that so many people lack access to basic necessities and that racism in America continues to lead to violence and injustice. I aspire to work toward a system that addresses these inequalities in the future. This summer I reflected back on all these things and have learned that no matter what, we all should continue to push on, even through hardships and obstacles.

Submit Your Story Online & WIN Prizes!!!

Student Name: Lillian Olson
Grade: 4

2020 Winning Story

Finding Fun during a Pandemic

This was a weird summer. We did not travel because of COVID-19 and stayed mostly at home and outside around our house. Even when I saw my friends, it was unusual. This summer, I worked and made money helping my parents.

The pandemic allowed me to spend more time inside and I learned many new skills. We made face masks and had to figure out which pattern fits us the best. My sister and I enjoyed creating other arts and crafts projects. Additionally, I have been learning to play instruments such as the piano, guitar, and trombone. We also baked and cooked because we did not go out to eat (at all!). I love baking desserts. The brownies and cookies we made were amazing! I also read for one hour a day and did a workbook by Lumos Learning. I especially loved Math.

Our time outdoors was different this summer. We ordered hens. My family spent a lot of time fixing the coop and setting it up for our 18 chickens. We had a daily responsibility to take care of our chickens in the morning, giving them food and water and in the evening, securing them in their coop. We were surprised that 3 of the hens were actually roosters! Additionally, we exhausted many days gardening and building a retaining wall. Our garden has many different fruits and vegetables. The retaining wall required many heavy bricks, shoveling rocks, and moving dirt around. To cool off from doing all this hard work, we jumped in a stream and went tubing. Our dog, Coco liked to join us.

COVID-19 has also caused me to interact differently with my friends. We used FaceTime, Zoom, and Messenger Kids to chat and video talk with each other. Video chatting is not as fun as being in person with my friends. I love Messenger Kids because it is fun and you can play interactive games with each other.

I had to spend some of my time working. I helped clean my parents' Airbnb. This was busier because of COVID-19. My sister and I will start to sell the chicken eggs once they start to lay which we expect to happen anytime. We had a small business two years ago doing this same thing.

Summer 2020 has been unusual in many ways. We played indoors and outdoors at our house and nearby with family. I have learned new skills and learned to use technology in different ways. Summer of 2020 will never be forgotten!

Submit Your Story Online & WIN Prizes!!!

Answer Key &
Detailed Explanations

Week 1

Question No.	Answer	Detailed Explanation
1	D	It requires multiplication to find out the amount for twice as many. The symbol for multiplication is x. If **n** represents Josh's age, then **a** represents Andrew's age.
2	B	Mandy is making 4 equal groups out of 28. Therefore, 28 divided by 4 equal the number of marbles each friend receives.
3	B	To find n, we need to get it alone by subtracting the other numbers. This is an equation that needs to stay balanced, so what is done on one side of the = sign must be done on the other side. If we subtract 9 (6+3) from both sides, we have n = 13.
4	6x4=24	Since there are 4 boxes, with 6 crayons in each box, to find the total number of crayons, multiply 4 and 6 together, which equals 24.
5	B	The second choice is correct. When Mary began reading her story to her class, those were the first words that she read. The title of a story goes at the top of the page, and those are the first words read when sharing a story aloud.
6	C	The third choice is correct. The passage states that "However, there was one part about every Friday at school that Mary did not enjoy, and that was when she had to share her story in front of the class."
7	C	The third choice is correct because the passage stated that, "The teacher made all of the children share on Friday afternoons."
8		Mom clapped loudly when she arrived at the hotel.

Day 2

Question No.	Answer	Detailed Explanation
1	C	Each box has 24 pears and there are 4 boxes, so that is 24 x 4, which equals 96.
2	D	The total collection is 450. Each page will have 15 cards or parts of the whole. When you divide 450 by 15, the answer tells how many pages are needed.
3	C	There are 12 dogs in Bow Wow Pet Shop. Since, each dog has 4 puppies, the total number of puppies will be 12 x 4 which is equal to 48.
4	$5	This is a two step problem. First, we divide the amount Charlie has ($938) by the number of his family members (15). This is a problem on division, in which the remainder has to be interpreted.
5	C	The third choice is correct. We know that the poet was surprised to hear a song from the shell, because the poet "listened hard, And it was really true." It makes sense to gather information before confirming a situation is true.
6	C	The third choice is correct. We know that the horse was scared, because the passage said "Realizing that the horse was terrified of its own shadow." Terrified means the same thing as scared.
7	D	The fourth choice is correct. We can infer that Cindy did not like what her mother had cooked, because she asked if she could cook something else (the frozen pizza).
8	A	The correct answer choice is A.

Question No.	Answer	Detailed Explanation
1	B	Round off the cost of the textbooks to the nearest dollar. $34.99 is close to $35.00. Round off the price of the backpack from $19.98 to $20.00. The estimated amount Kristian paid can be found by calculating 4 x $35.00 + $20.00. 4 x $35.00 = $140.00; $140.00 + 20.00 = $160.00
2	C	To find the estimated total, round each number to the nearest thousand, then add. 14,667 rounds to 15,000; 16,992 rounds to 17,000; and 18,124 rounds to 18,000. 15,000 + 17,000 + 18,000 = 50,000
3	B	To decide which choice is true, use estimation. Steven has filled about 150 pages in his album. (147 is close to 150.) There are about 10 cards on each page. Therefore, he has about 1,500 cards. (150 x 10 = 1,500) Since both of the numbers were rounded up, this estimate is an overestimate. Steven, therefore, has slightly less than 1,500 cards. The second choice is the most reasonable.
4	$22	Amount Charlie earned by selling 8 large paintings = 8 x 35 = $280. We subtract this amount from his total earnings ($412) to find the selling price of 6 small paintings; 412 - 280 = $132. Selling price of 1 small painting = m; Selling price of 6 small paintings = 6 x m = 132. Therefore, m = 132 ÷ 6 = $22
5	C	The third choice is correct. Fred spent a lot of time worrying about visiting the dentist and got himself really worked up. When he actually visited the dentist, nothing bad happened to him. He realized that he did not need to worry.
6	B	The second choice is correct. Opal felt really bad when she acted dishonestly. After she told the truth, she instantly felt better.
7	A	The first choice is correct. The quilt did not cost much money, but it had a lot of sentimental value to Libby.
8	D	Sea Shell Song is the best title, because the main idea of the passage is "a girl discovered that a shell has a song."

Question No.	Answer	Detailed Explanation
1	C	Multiples are the products of two numbers. Skip count, recite time-tables or refer to a chart to find all of the multiples of both numbers, from 1 to 100. Listing these multiples may also be helpful: 10 is 10, 20, 30, 40, 50, 60, 70, etc. 4 is 4, 8, 12, 16, 20, 24, 28, 32, etc. All of the multiples of 10 will have an x and all of multiples of 4 will be circled. The question to the problem is **how many numbers will have an x, but** *not* **be circled.** In the list of 10 multiples, circle all the multiples of 4. Count the number of multiples of 10 that do not have a circle.
2	C	The multiple of 30 must be a product of 30 x another number. 60 = 30 x 2.
3	B	In this diagram, Section A would contain the multiples of 8 which are not multiples of 3. Section C would contain the multiples of 3 which are not multiples of 8. Section B would contain multiples of both 8 and 3. Section D would list numbers that are **not** multiples of 8 or 3. 8 x 9 = 72 and 3 x 24 = 72, so 72 would be found in Section B.
4	A,C&D	Multiples of 8 : There are 10 numbers up to 80 (8, 16, etc.) which are divisible by 8. There are 2 numbers between 81 to 100 which are divisible by 8 (88 and 96). Therefore, there are 12 numbers between 1 and 100 which are divisible by 8. Therefore, option (A) is correct. Multiples of 6 : There are 10 numbers up to 60 (6, 12, etc.) which are divisible by 6. There are 6 numbers between 61 to 100 which are divisible by 6 (66, 72, 78, 84, 90, 96). So, there are 16 numbers between 1 and 100 which are divisible by 6. Among the multiples of 8, 4 numbers (24, 48, 72 and 96) are divisible by 6. Therefore, there are 12 - 4 = 8 numbers that are circled but do not have X on them. Therefore, option (B) is wrong. 24, 48, 72 and 96 are divisible by both 6 and 8. Therefore, option (C) is correct. Among the multiples of 6, 4 numbers (24, 48, 72 and 96) are divisible by 8. Therefore, there are 16 - 4 = 12 numbers which have X on them but are not circled. Therefore, option (D) is correct.

Question No.	Answer	Detailed Explanation
5	B	The second choice is correct, because it tells only the important information from the passage. Option D also gives a summary, but it has additional information that is not needed.
6	A	The first choice is correct, because it tells only the most important information from the passage. Options B. and C do not give enough information. Option D basically retells the entire story instead of just summarizing it.
7	A	The first choice is correct, because it gives only the most important information from the passage. Some of the information in the other answer choices is out of order. Options B and D do not summarize because there is too much information.
8	A	Answer choice A is correct. This answer gives the most detail and is found in the passage.

Question No.	Answer	Detailed Explanation
1	A	Identify whether there is adding, subtracting multiplying or dividing to create this pattern. If the numbers increase, it is adding or multiplying; if the numbers decrease, it is subtracting or dividing. The next thing is to determine the relationship between the numbers in the pattern, starting with the first two: 26 and 39 is an increase. Ask yourself: Is the increase from adding or multiplying. If the numbers are multiples of a number or numbers, the increase is from multiplying. Otherwise, it is from adding. How many numbers are between 26 and 39 is the answer to how many numbers are being added. Be sure to read the question carefully.
2	B	The numbers are increasing, so determine if this pattern is adding or multiplying. The numbers in the problem are multiples of 7, so a continued list of the multiples of 7 are needed to continue this pattern.
3	D	Carefully read each answer choice and check the given numbers. Ascending means increasing and descending means decreasing. Even numbers are all numbers that are multiples of 2. Multiples of 50,000 would be any numbers that are products of 50,000 x another whole number. In this problem, the numbers are increasing (not decreasing), even, and they are multiples of 25,000. Therefore, statements made in options (A), (B), and (C) are true. But all the numbers are not multiples of 50,000. For example, 1,25,000 / 50,000 = 2.5. Therefore, statement made in option (D) is not true. We have to choose the statement which is not true. So, option (D) is the correct answer.
4	D	For each number in the IN column, the corresponding number in the OUT column is less. Therefore, check whether you get the number in the OUT column by subtracting or dividing the number in the IN column. Also to be considered is what could be done to 72 to get 8. If we divide 72 by 9, we get 8. Now, check whether this rule "divide by 9" holds for the other two numbers also. $63 \div 9 = 7$, $45 \div 9 = 5$. The rule "divide by 9" holds good in all the three cases.

Question No.	Answer	Detailed Explanation
5	C	The third choice is correct. We know that Timothy is responsible, because the passage reads that he gets up early every day to perform his dog walking job. We know that Timothy is ambitious, because Timothy believes he can continue his dog walking job and participate in extracurricular activities.
6	B	The second answer is correct. We know that Timothy wouldn't help someone cheat on a test. The passage indicates that "he is always honest and expects others to be honest."
7	B	The second choice is correct. We know that Fred was afraid and didn't understand the reason that he had to go to the dentist. The passage states that he had heard horror stories about the dentist and he thought the dentist would torture him. The passage reads that he didn't understand the reason that his mom thought he needed to go since his teeth weren't hurting.
8	B, C	Answer B and C are correct. These are characteristics found in the passage. She was spoiled, selfish, ill-tempered and tyrannical.

Question No.	Answer	Detailed Explanation
1	A	Place values are read from right to left, beginning with the "ones" place, "tens", "hundreds", "thousands", "ten thousands", "hundred thousands", "millions", etc. If you were to write the number in the boxes below, you see the 9 is in the ten-thousand column.

Place Value Chart

Hundred-billions	Ten-billions	Billions	Hundred-millions	Ten-millions	Millions	Hundred-thousands	Ten-thousands	Thousands	Hundreds	Tens	Ones

Question No.	Answer	Detailed Explanation
2	D	Begin naming the place values for each number from the right. Number 9 is in the ten thousands place. Place values increase by multiplying 10: 1 ten is 10, 10 tens is a hundred, 10 hundreds is a thousand, etc.
3	A	Multiply 9 x 10,000 to find 90,000.

4

	5	50	500
How many hundreds are in 500?	●		
How many tens are in 500?		●	
How many ones are in 500?			●

Question No.	Answer	Detailed Explanation
5	A	The first choice is correct. The first sentence of the passage tells us that the story takes place two thousand five hundred years ago.
6	B	The second choice is correct. The setting for the second paragraph is an automobile, because it tells us that Fred and his mother were on their way to the dentist.
7	A	The first choice is correct. Huckleberry Hound was in the yard at the beginning of the story. The first sentence of the passage provides this information.
8	B,C & D	Answer B, C and D are correct options. These are all noted in the passage.

Week 2

Question No.	Answer	Detailed Explanation
1	D	Ascending order is from least to greatest value. All of these numbers start in the ten thousands place, however the numbers beginning with a 2 have a lesser value. If the numbers are the same in the thousands place, for example, compare the numbers that are different in the hundreds place. If the digits are the same in the hundreds place, compare the tens.
2	B	6 hundreds, 2 tens and 4 ones is greater than 2 hundreds, 6 tens and 4 ones. The numbers are the same in all places above the ten places so you have to look there.
3	B	8 x 10 is greater than 7 x 10.

Question 4

	<	>	=
4,145 ___ 4,451	●		
31,600 __ 63,100	●		
49 _____ 49			●
831 _____ 381		●	

We need to compare the numbers and fill in with the correct sign. < means less than, > means greater than, and = means equals.

For the first two, we see that the first number is smaller than the second, so < would fit. The third line has equal numbers, so we would choose =. Finally, the last set of numbers has the first one being the larger, so we would choose >.

Question No.	Answer	Detailed Explanation
5	C	The third choice is correct. We know that Timothy is saving up for youth camp, because the last sentence of the passage tells us so.
6	B	The second choice is correct. We know that Timothy gets up at 5 a.m. to walk dogs, because the third sentence of the second paragraph provides the time.
7	C	The third choice is correct. We know that Fred is worried about going to the dentist because people who are scared often tremble.
8		The events that led to the parade was firstly they rode the trolly and got free breakfast. secondly, they were able to go to the splash mountain, jungle cruise, the seven dwarfs mine train and much more. Finally, they saw the parade on the side of the castle because the hotel clerk told the mother how to find a good seat to view the parade.

Day 3

Question No.	Answer	Detailed Explanation
1	D	Since this number is to be rounded to the nearest hundred, the number to the right of the hundreds place (the tens place) will determine if the hundreds digit is to be rounded up to the next number or stay the same. If the number in the tens place is 0-4, keep the hundreds place the same. If the number in the tens place is between 5 and 9 (inclusive), round the hundred up to the next number. Example 678 would round up to 700; whereas 628 would round down to 600.
2	C	The number in the hundreds place is a 1, so the thousands place will not change. It will remain a zero. The hundreds, tens, and ones places will also become zeros.
3	B	Use the digit in the thousands place to decide how to round. In this number, the thousands place has a zero, so the ten thousands place will remain unchanged when rounding.
4	A	The given number is between 750,000 and 760,000. When rounding is done, it is rounded to 760,000. Therefore, the number is rounded up. It means the number has to be more than 755,000. Therefore, the digit in the thousands place has to be 5 or more than 5. Therefore, option (A) is correct.
5	D	"Twinkled like diamonds" is a simile. A simile compares two things using like or as. The way the girl's eyes twinkle is being compared to how diamonds twinkle.
6	B	This is a metaphor. A metaphor is a direct comparison of two unlike objects. Her heart is being compared to stone. Stone is hard, and her heart was hard (meaning she was not very sensitive).
7	C	This is a metaphor. The sound the bird made was being compared to music, meaning it made a pleasant, entertaining sound.

8

	germ (inner layer)	endosperm (middle layer)	bran (outer layer)
the weight of the grain		●	
the fiber			●
unsaturated fats	●		

Question No.	Answer	Detailed Explanation
1	B	Any number plus 0 is always that number, so 0 is the additive identity.
2	A	The Commutative Property means that changing the order of the addends (the two numbers being added together) does not change the sum.
3	D	Adding a negative number is the same as subtracting it. For example, 6 + -6 is the same as 6 - 6. Also, 10 and -10 are additive inverses, so their sum must be the additive identity, 0.
4	C	$$\begin{array}{r} 4927 \\ +5098 \\ \hline 10,025 \end{array}$$
5	D	The Three Little Pigs is told in sequence or chronologically. The events are told in the order that they happened.
6	D	Descriptive texts tell the characteristics of a particular subject.
7	D	This is a narrative text, because the writer is describing an event in his or her life.
8	A & C	These sentences intrigue the reader to want to read more.

Question No.	Answer	Detailed Explanation
1	B	Apply the rule to each IN value: 8 x 6
2	D	This problem could be solved using the Distributive Property: 26 x 8 = (20 + 6) x 8 = (20 x 8) + (6 x 8) = 160 + 48 = 208
3	B	Any number times 1 will always equal that number.
4	7,290	Monday through Friday is 5 days. Multiply 1,458 by 5 to get the total distance traveled. Total distance traveled = 1,458 x 5 = (1,000 + 400 + 50 + 8) x 5 = 1,000 x 5 + 400 x 5 + 50 x 5 + 8 x 5 = 5,000 + 2,000 + 250 + 40 = 7,290 miles
5	B	Second person point of view is when the writer is talking directly to the reader.
6	A	First person point of view is when one of the characters is telling the story. Pronouns such as I and me are used.
7	C	Third person point of view is when the story is told by someone who is not a character in the story.
8		The Bengal Tiger is an endangered species, due to habit loss and deforestation. This animal concerns me most because there are only 2,00 Bengal Tigers left in the wild. Their population is declining due to illegal poaching and there is a demand in the market for their skins, nails, and tooth. Also, their hunting grounds is reducing year after year, due to deforestation. In China, Tigers are bred in captivity and killed for their organs for their cuisine. Due to man's intervention in the forest, their reproduction is also on the decline and they get frequent diseases.

Question No.	Answer	Detailed Explanation
1	C	The number that follows the division symbol (÷) is called the divisor.
2	C	91 ÷ 7 will have no remainder, since 91 is a multiple of 7. 7 x 13 = 91.
3	B	Count the value of the base 10 blocks that are shown, which is 352. Because there is only one set of blocks, regroup each hundreds flat into 10 tens rods. Regroup each tens rod into ten ones cubes. Place 1 tens rod and 1 ones cube into 2 groups until all are placed. Count the value of the tens blocks shown in both groups. The numbers should be the same.
4		(see table below)
5	B	The picture of the female in front of a chalkboard is appropriate, because this story takes place in a school classroom and Mary is speaking to her class.
6	C	The third choice is correct, because it is about baby monkeys. There are baby monkeys in the picture.
7	C	The third choice is correct, because it is about a kitten at a construction site. The kitten in the picture is in a concrete pipe.
8	6; 4; +2	The pattern on the table shows each game the score decreases by 2 points for both teams, but the Blue Jets still win with +2 over the other teams.

Question 4:

Dividend	Divisor	Quotient	Remainder
128	8	16	0
435	7	**62**	**1**
350	6	**58**	**2**

Question 8:

Game #	Team Blue Jets	Opposing Team	Difference + or -
1	10	8	+2
2	8	6	+2
3	**6**	**4**	**+2**

Day 2

Question No.	Answer	Detailed Explanation
1	C	The denominator (bottom number) is the total number of items presented. The numerator (top number) is the number of identified items.
2	C	There are three different shapes represented. This question is asking for the number of squares and triangles. That number of shapes that are not circles is the numerator and the total number of shapes is the denominator.
3	A	The fraction should only pertain to the number of squares: the number of shaded squares is the numerator and the total number of squares is the denominator.
4	$\frac{4}{5}$	30 is the GCF of 120 and 150. When the GCF is taken out from both the numerator and denominator, 120/150 reduces to $\frac{4}{5}$.
5	C	The third choice is correct, because it most accurately describes how Fred was afraid at first and then relieved after he saw the dentist.
6	C	The third choice is correct, because it tells a way that the two boys are alike. Compare means to tell how one or more subjects are alike.
7	D	To contrast means to tell how two subjects are different. The fourth choice tells what both Stanley and Timothy like to do.
8		Answer may vary

Question No.	Answer	Detailed Explanation
1	C	Point D is located halfway between -1 and -2 on the number line. This point would represent -1.5, or $-1\frac{1}{2}$.
2	A	All of these fractions are equivalent because they reduce to the same fraction when reduced to lowest terms. They would all reduce to $\frac{2}{7}$.
3	C	Both fractions are showing three parts. $\frac{3}{12}$ is 3 parts out of 12; $\frac{3}{18}$ is 3 parts out of 18. The greater the denominator, the more pieces the wholes have been divided into. Therefore, the pieces will be smaller.
4	B & C	To compare two fractions, we write equivalent fractions of them which have the same numerator or denominator. $\frac{3}{5} < \frac{4}{5}$ (When a whole is divided into 5 equal parts, 3 parts are less than 4 parts). Therefore, option (A) is wrong. $\frac{1}{5} > \frac{1}{10}$. Because $\frac{1}{5}$ is one part when the whole is divided into 5 equal parts and $\frac{1}{10}$ is one part when the congruent whole is divided into 10 equal parts. Since $5 < 10$, $\frac{1}{5} > \frac{1}{10}$. So, 3 fifths ($\frac{3}{5}$) is more than 3 tenths ($\frac{3}{10}$). $\frac{3}{5} > \frac{3}{10}$. Therefore, option (B) is correct. $\frac{3}{5} = \frac{3\times3}{5\times3} = \frac{9}{15}$. $\frac{9}{15} > \frac{8}{15}$ (When a whole is divided into 15 equal parts, 9 parts are more than 8 parts). or $\frac{3}{5} > \frac{8}{15}$. Therefore, option (C) is correct. $\frac{3}{5} = \frac{3\times4}{5\times4} = \frac{12}{20}$. Therefore, option (D) is wrong.
5	D	The fourth answer choice is correct. The author says the ostrich, "cannot fly," and that, "it can travel faster by running." Traveling faster is an advantage for the ostrich.
6	D	The fourth answer choice is correct. By saying, "one of their favorite companions," the author implies the ostrich has many companions. The ostrich is not shy and solitary if it has many companions.
7	A	"Solitary" means alone. The first answer choice is correct because the statement contrasts the blue whale's behavior with the behavior of other whales that live in pods.
8	C	The third choice is correct. Although the letter is polite, Tim West was displeased with his experience. Only dissatisfied customers ask for refunds.

Question No.	Answer	Detailed Explanation
1	A	To determine how many pounds of apples he has left, subtract the amount of apples he gave away from the amount of apples he picked. Break this into two smaller subtraction problems, beginning with the whole numbers. Angelo had 2 full pounds of apples, and gave 1 full pound away: $2-1=1$. He now has 1 full pound of apples. In addition to the 2 full pounds, he had 3/4 of a pound of apples, and gave $\frac{1}{4}$ of a pound away: $\frac{3}{4}-\frac{1}{4}=\frac{2}{4}$. He now has $\frac{2}{4}$ of a pound of apples in addition to the 1 full pound of apples. All together, Angelo has $1\frac{2}{4}$ pounds of apples left. This can be reduced to $1\frac{1}{2}$ pounds.
2	D	$1\frac{3}{4}+1\frac{1}{4}=1+\frac{3}{4}+1+\frac{1}{4}$. Using the Commutative Property of Addition, we have $1+\frac{3}{4}+1+\frac{1}{4}=1+1+\frac{3}{4}+\frac{1}{4}$. We can then simply add the whole numbers together and add the fractions together. Adding the whole numbers we have $1 + 1 = 2$. Adding the fractions we have $\frac{3}{4} + \frac{1}{4} = \frac{4}{4} = 1$. Together we have $2+1=3$. Combined, the boys have 3 buckets of plastic building blocks.
3	D	The amount of chocolate chips needed can be expressed in number of fractional pieces ($\frac{17}{4}$), or number of wholes, and additional fractional pieces ($4\frac{1}{4}$). This task requires an understanding of comparing fractions or mixed numbers. Combine $2\frac{3}{4}$ and $1\frac{3}{4}$. $2 + 1 = 3$ and $\frac{3}{4} + \frac{3}{4} = \frac{6}{4} = 1\frac{2}{4}$. The combined total of chips will be $4\frac{2}{4}$ cups. Because $4\frac{2}{4}$ is greater than $4\frac{1}{4}$, Lexi and Ava will have enough chocolate chips for their cookies. $4\frac{2}{4}$ can be reduced to $4\frac{1}{2}$.

Question No.	Answer	Detailed Explanation

4

	2	$3\frac{3}{4}$	$4\frac{1}{4}$
$2\frac{1}{4} + 1\frac{2}{4}$		◉	
$5\frac{1}{4} - 2\frac{3}{4}$	◉		
$2\frac{3}{4} + 1\frac{2}{4}$			◉

First, add the whole numbers together, and then add the fractions. To add fractions, you first have to have the denominator the same. After that, add the numerators and keep the denominator the same. Finally, reduce if possible. Subtraction: First, look at the fractions, and see if you have to regroup. Then subtract the fractions, by making sure you have the same denominator, subtracting the numerators, and keeping the denominator the same. Finally, subtract the whole numbers.

Question No.	Answer	Detailed Explanation
5	B	Resonating means loud, because the passage says that their resonating sound makes them the loudest animal on earth.
6	B	An herbivore is an animal that eats only plants. The passage gives us a clue when it describes that the plants dying caused the herbivores to die.
7	D	Carnivores are animals that eat meat.
8	C	Favorable means positive. The clue is that people enjoyed it.

Question No.	Answer	Detailed Explanation
1	B	The amount of pizza Marcie ate can be thought of a $\frac{3}{6}$ (or $\frac{1}{6}$ and $\frac{1}{6}$ and $\frac{1}{6}$). The amount of pizza Lisa ate can be thought of a $\frac{1}{6}$ and $\frac{1}{6}$. The total amount of pizza they ate is $\frac{1}{6} + \frac{1}{6} + \frac{1}{6} + \frac{1}{6} + \frac{1}{6}$ or $\frac{5}{6}$ of the whole pizza.
2	D	The ribbon Sophie has can be added to the ribbon Angie has to determine how much ribbon they have altogether. Sophie has $3\frac{1}{8}$ feet of ribbon and Angie has $5\frac{3}{8}$ feet of ribbon. This can be written as $3\frac{1}{8} + 5\frac{3}{8}$. You add the 3 and 5, and they also have $\frac{1}{8}$ and $\frac{3}{8}$ which makes a total of $\frac{4}{8}$ more. Altogether the girls have $8\frac{4}{8}$ feet of ribbon, $8\frac{4}{8}$ is less than $8\frac{5}{8}$ so they will not have enough ribbon to complete the project. They will be short by $\frac{1}{8}$ of a foot of ribbon.
3	B	Travis had $4\frac{1}{8}$ pizzas to start. This is $\frac{33}{8}$ of a pizza. The x's show the pizza he has left which is $2\frac{4}{8}$ pizzas or $\frac{20}{8}$ pizzas. The shaded rectangles without the x's are the pizza he gave to his friend which is $\frac{13}{8}$ or $1\frac{5}{8}$ pizzas.
4	A & D	This is a problem on addition of fractions. First, express the fractions in terms of the least common denominator(LCD). Add the whole numbers and fractions separately and then put them together. LCD fo 3 and 4 is 12. $\frac{1}{3} = \frac{1\times4}{3\times4} = \frac{4}{12}; \frac{1}{4} = \frac{1\times3}{4\times3} = \frac{3}{12}$
5	D	Descriptive text structures give characteristics of a particular topic in no particular order.
6	B	Compare/contrast passages tell how subjects are alike and different.
7	D	The text structure is sequence, because the steps are given in the order that they occurred.
8	C	This would be narrative writing, because it tells about a personal experience from a first-person point of view.

Question No.	Answer	Detailed Explanation
1	C	Multiply $\frac{1}{2} \times \frac{6}{1}$. The answer is a fraction in which the numerator is larger than the denominator. This is called an improper fraction, which is always reduced to its lowest terms by dividing the denominator into the numerator: $\frac{6}{2}$. The quotient will be a whole number if there is no remainder. This is the answer.
2	B	The first answer is an improper fraction that, when divided into the numerator, has a remainder. Therefore, the answer will be a mixed fraction-a whole number and a fraction. The whole number represents how many times the denominator divides into the numerator. The remainder represents the numerator in the fraction and the denominator is the same denominator of the improper fraction in the original problem. Fraction part may be reduced to its simplest form. $6 \times \frac{1}{4} = (\frac{6}{1}) \times (\frac{1}{4}) = \frac{6 \times 1}{1 \times 4} = \frac{6}{4} = 1\frac{2}{4} = 1\frac{1}{2}$
3	D	One Whole + One Whole and later on multiply with $\frac{7}{10}$. $= 2 \times \frac{7}{10} = \frac{14}{10}$ Convert to mixed fraction $= 1\frac{4}{10}$
4	A, C & D	$5 \times \frac{2}{7} - \frac{5}{1} \times \frac{2}{7} - \frac{5 \times 2}{1 \times 7} = \frac{10}{7}$. Therefore, option A is correct. $\frac{10}{7} - 1\frac{3}{7}$. Therefore, option C is correct. $5 \times \frac{2}{7}$ means adding $\frac{2}{7}$ five times. Therefore, option D is correct.
5	D	The fourth choice is correct. The first hand account is by the baton twirler and is limited to her personal experiences and observations. The second hand account covers the observations about the entire parade by the reporter.
6	D	The fourth choice is correct. There is information in both texts about the weather, the marching band, the baton twirlers, and the crowd. The other answer choices only appear in one of the two accounts.
7	A	The first choice is correct. We learn in the firsthand account that the narrator is embarrassed by the events during the parade, while the secondhand account omits emotions and includes mostly facts about the parade.
8		Third person point of view is when the story is being told by a person who is not a character in the story.

Question No.	Answer	Detailed Explanation
1	D	To multiply a whole number by a unit fraction, multiply the whole number by 1 to get the numerator in the product. The denominator will not change.
2	B	Add up all of the fractional parts of meat. $\frac{2}{8} + \frac{2}{8} + \frac{2}{8} + \frac{2}{8} + \frac{2}{8} = \frac{10}{8}$ pounds. Then convert the improper fraction to a mixed number: 1 $\frac{2}{8}$ or $1\frac{1}{4}$ pounds.
3	A	To multiply a whole number by a unit fraction, multiply the whole number by 1 to get the numerator in the product. The denominator will not change.
4	8	We can solve this by guess and check if we want. To multiply a fraction by a whole number we multiply the numerator by the whole number, and leave the denominator alone. For example, we can pick and try 10. ½ x 10 = 5, which is too big but we are close to 4. So we can try 8. $\frac{1}{2}$ x 8 = 4, so we know the missing number is 8.
5	D	The fourth answer choice is correct. The chart makes the details clear by categorizing them according to tissue type. It does not add information or elaborate, but rather makes the information more concise. It does not change details.
6	D	The fourth answer choice is correct. The chart makes it easy to see that both muscle tissue and nerve tissue have long cells.
7	B	Microscopic views of each tissue type would show the reader exactly what each type looks like and how they are different.
8		A map of The United States shows different places such as important states, cities, towns, etc., but a geological map shows rivers, mountains, types of rocks, etc.,

Day 5

Question No.	Answer	Detailed Explanation
1	B	Students may use the multiplication equation $9 \times \frac{2}{3} = \frac{18}{3}$ or 6 cups of mint M&Ms. Students may use the repeated addition equation $\frac{2}{3} + \frac{2}{3} + \frac{2}{3} + \frac{2}{3} + \frac{2}{3} + \frac{2}{3} + \frac{2}{3} + \frac{2}{3} + \frac{2}{3} = \frac{18}{3}$ or 6 cups of mint M&Ms.
2	A	Students could have used: $9 \times \frac{1}{2} = \frac{9}{2}$ or $4\frac{1}{2}$ cups of coconut M&Ms. Or, students could have used: $\frac{1}{2} + \frac{1}{2} + \frac{1}{2} + \frac{1}{2} + \frac{1}{2} + \frac{1}{2} + \frac{1}{2} + \frac{1}{2} + \frac{1}{2} = \frac{9}{2}$ or $4\frac{1}{2}$ cups of coconut M&Ms.
3	B	Student may draw a model that shows that $\frac{2}{3} + \frac{1}{2} > 1$. Student may state that $\frac{2}{3}$ is more than $\frac{1}{2}$. If $\frac{1}{2} + \frac{1}{2} = 1$, then $\frac{2}{3} + \frac{1}{2} > 1$. Student may convert fractions to common denominators and add to find the total is $\frac{7}{6}$ or $1\frac{1}{6}$ cups of M&Ms.
4	D	Multiply 8 by $\frac{2}{5}$ to get the number of tables Jose can paint. $8 \times \frac{2}{5} = \frac{8 \times 2}{5} = \frac{16}{5} = 3\frac{1}{5}$. Jose can paint $3\frac{1}{5}$ tables in 15 minutes.
5	C	The third choice is correct. It gives specific details about the size and weight of the blue whale's body.
6	C	The third choice tells specifically how the whales communicate.
7	C	The third choice is correct. The picture is evidence that the package arrived damaged..
8	B	The main idea is for kids to exercise. The entire passage is about exploring this concept.

Question No.	Answer	Detailed Explanation
1	A	6 dimes is 60 pennies, so 6 dimes and 3 pennies is 63 pennies, which is $\frac{63}{100}=0.63$ of a dollar

2	A	

thousands	hundreds	tens	units	• decimal	tenths	hundredths	thousandths	ten thousandths
					1	4		

0.14 is read as 14 hundredths ($\frac{14}{100}$).

3	C	

thousands	hundreds	tens	units	• decimal	tenths	hundredths	thousandths	ten thousandths
					5	2		

0.52 is read as 52 hundredths $\frac{52}{100}$

4		

	$\frac{10}{100}$	$\frac{60}{100}$	$\frac{90}{100}$
$\frac{9}{10}$			◉
$\frac{1}{10}$	◉		
$\frac{6}{10}$		◉	

To find equivalent fractions, you have to multiply the numerator and denominator by the same number. In this case, we want to get the denominator to 100, so we have to multiply each by 10

5	D	The fourth answer choice is correct. The first three choices include only information from one of the texts. The fourth choice integrates information from both texts.
6	B	The second choice is correct. Information from the other three choices are not found in the texts.
7	A	The first choice is correct. This is the only choice with a pair of sentences from each text that means essentially the same thing. When doing research, one should look for similar information found in multiple texts, as this adds to its validity.
8	C	The third choice is correct. The first choice is untrue, and the second choice asserts the volcano theory as fact, disregarding any discussion of a meteorite.

Question No.	Answer	Detailed Explanation
1	C	Point A is located near $\frac{1}{4}$ of 1 on the number line. In order to represent numbers that are less than 1, a fraction or decimal is used. To convert the fraction to a decimal, divide the numerator by the denominator, adding zeros until there is no remainder. A decimal point is plotted after the last digit in the dividend. Another decimal point is plotted directly above that one in the answer. The decimal equivalent of $\frac{1}{4}$ is 0.25.
2	A	This fraction would be read "one hundred forty-eight thousandths." As a decimal, that number is written 0.148.
3	C	Point D is halfway between -1 and -2. Halfway between -1 and -2 is -1.5.
4	A, C & D	$\frac{6}{10}$ is read as 6 tenths. Here, the denominator is 10. Therefore, we can directly write the numerator putting the decimal in the correct spot (one space from the right-hand side for every zero in the denominator); 0.6 Therefore, option (A) is correct. $\frac{6}{10} = \frac{6 \times 10}{10 \times 10} = \frac{60}{100}$ Multiply and divide 0.06 by 100 to remove the decimal point. $0.06 = \frac{0.06 \times 100}{100} = \frac{6.00}{100} = \frac{6}{100}$. $\frac{6}{100}$ is not equal to $\frac{6}{10}$. Therefore, option (B) is wrong. Therefore, option (C) is correct. 0.60 is the same as 0.6 (the zero at the end of 0.60 has no value.) Therefore, option (D) is correct.
5	B	'We' refers to Bobby and the author. While 'us' could also refer to both Bobby and the author, it is not the correct pronoun for this set of sentences.
6	C	His is a possessive pronoun referring to something belonging to the father.
7	A	'He' refers to Jamie which makes it the correct pronoun in this sentence.
8	D	Since the sentence contains the word together, we know that more than one person is involved.

Week 5

Question No.	Answer	Detailed Explanation
1	A	The point is plotted at about $1\frac{3}{4}$. Convert this mixed fraction to a decimal. $1\frac{3}{4} = 1.75$
2	A	0.05 is 5 hundredths. 0.50 is 50 hundredths. $0.05 < 0.50$
3	B	All of the dinner prices consist of decimals that have numbers to the left of the decimal point. Those numbers are whole numbers (dollars). To compare, simply look at the dollar amounts. The cents do not matter as long as the dollar amounts are all different. Note: The cost of the chicken dinner is \$25.79. (30.79 - 5.00 = 25.79)

Question 4

	<	>	=
0.25 _ 0.39	◯		
0.89 _ 0.890			◯
0.12 _ 0.21	◯		
0.29 _ 0.28		◯	

To compare decimals, look at each digit individually. Looking at the tenths digit, if they are different, the one with the larger number in the tenths place is the larger number. If the tenths are the same, move one digit to the right, and repeat that process with the hundredths place. If there is a zero in the last digit like in row two, those numbers are still equivalent, because you can drop the zero.

Question No.	Answer	Detailed Explanation
5	B	Efrain is the subject of the sentence. Since he will be traveling to Europe in the future, the future progressive tense is correct.
6	D	Darrel and I are the subjects of the sentence. Since there is a plural subject, 'will attend' is the correct verb.
7	A	Since Minnie, Jill, and Sandra are singing presently, use the present progressive tense.
8	C	Kenji and Briana's parents will pick them up in the future, so future progressive tense is appropriate.

Question No.	Answer	Detailed Explanation
1	A	Inches are not units of weight. Kilograms are not customary units. Tons are too large to use to measure a table. Pounds are the best choice.
2	B	Grams are not customary units. Between ounces and pounds, ounces are more reasonable unit to use.
3	A	12 lbs = 1.5 - 2 times a newborn baby. Gallons are used for liquid measurement. 200 ounces is only 12.5 pounds. 500 pounds is the most reasonable choice.
4		

	4	5	6
360 min = ___ hr			●
500 cm = ___ m		●	
240 sec = ___ min	●		

We know that there are 60 min in an hour, so we divide 360 by 60 to get the value for 360 min, which is 6 hours. We know there are 100 cm in 1 meter, so we divide 500 by 100 to get the value for 500 cm, which is 5 meters. We know there are 60 seconds in 1 min, so we divide 240 by 60 to get the value for 240 seconds, which is 4 minutes.

Question No.	Answer	Detailed Explanation
5	D	"Will" in sentence 3 and "may" in sentence 4 are both modal auxiliary verbs. These modal auxiliaries are connected to ideas of doubt or probability of future events.
6	B	Modal auxiliaries can be used for each of these purposes; but in this case it is uncertain whether or not Oliver's fever will go away.
7	D	"Could" is the correct answer choice. It is being used to express a past possibility.
8	C	"Had" is the modal auxiliary verb. It is being used to affirm that Dana had no choice about leaving the party.

Question No.	Answer	Detailed Explanation
1	B	To determine the difference between the time Arthur wants to arrive at practice and how long it takes him to get there, subtract 45 minutes from 5:30 by counting backwards by 5's on the clock:
2	A	Correct answer is 9:43 PM. Add 2 hours to 7:05, which would make 9:05. Count forward by 5's on the face of a clock for 35 minutes, then add 3 more minutes to determine the exact time
3	B	There are 12 inches in 1 foot: Multiply 12 x 4, and then and add 5 more inches.
4	3	2 cups goes into 6 cups 3 times, so the answer is 3.
5	C	Frequently is the adverb modifying 'visits'. It answers the question when.
6	B	Beautiful modifies park. It answers the question what kind.
7	D	Cold is an adjective in the sentence. It is modifying 'it'.
8	B	Fastest is the superlative adjective that completes the sentence.

Day 1

Question No.	Answer	Detailed Explanation
1	B	The formula for finding the area of a rectangle: Area = length x width.
2	A	The formula to find the perimeter of a rectangle: P = 2(length) + 2(width)
3	C	The length is 36 ft. and the width is 48 ft.. All sides must be added to determine the perimeter. Add 48 + 36. Then multiply the sum by 2.
4	20	To find the perimeter, add all the sides together. Since it is a rectangle, the 2 long sides are both 6, and the two short sides are 4. 6 + 6 + 4 + 4 = 20.
5	B	"Into the pool" and "of cool water" are both prepositional phrases.
6	D	"Underneath" is the preposition. Journals is the object of the preposition.
7	C	"For school" and "without your lunchbox" are both prepositional phrases.
8	D	There is no prepositional phrase in the fourth choice.

Week 6

Question No.	Answer	Detailed Explanation
1	D	The horizontal scale represents the number of cousins each student has. Read the number of xs plotted for 0 cousins.
2	C	Count the number of xs plotted above the number 4 on the horizontal scale.
3	B	The 2 foods that have the highest number of xs are the most favorites.

Question 4

	Bar graph	Line graph	Pie Chart
The results of the number of boys in each grade.	●		
The percentage of favorite desserts of the students in the class			●
The price of a car over the years.		●	

Bar graphs are best when looking at numbers in different categories, so that would be best used for counting the number of boys in each grade. Line graphs are best when looking at trends over a time span, so that would be best used for looking at the price of cars. Pie charts are best when looking at percentages, so that should be used when looking at the percentages of the favorite desserts.

Question No.	Answer	Detailed Explanation
5	A	The first answer choice makes the run-on sentence into a compound sentence by adding a comma and the coordinating conjunction, "but." This is appropriate because both parts of the sentence have a subject and predicate.
6	B	The second choice is correct. This resolves the run-on sentence by creating a compound sentence followed by a second complete sentence with a subject and predicate.
7	C	The third answer choice is correct. All of the other sentences have subjects and predicates, but the third choice is a dependent clause.
8	C	The third answer choice is correct. As is, the sentence doesn't have a verb. The subject is "ways." Adding "There are," gives this sentence a verb and makes it complete.

Day 3

Question No.	Answer	Detailed Explanation
1	B	Angle C and Angle A are congruent. They have the same exact measurements
2	A	Angle C and Angle D are supplementary. Their measures total 180°. 180 - 128 = 52
3	D	Angle B and Angle D are congruent so they will measure the same.
4	90	Since we know it is a right angle, we know it is 90 degrees
5	A	The first answer choice is correct. "Their" shows ownership.
6	C	The third choice is correct. "There" refers to a place.
7	B	The second answer choice is correct. The contraction, "they're" means "they are."
8	B	The second choice is correct. The principal is the leader of a school. A principle is a commonly held truth.

Week 6

Question No.	Answer	Detailed Explanation
1	B	A half-turn would be 180 degrees. Erika made a 180 degree turn, but her goal was 360 degrees. 360-180= 180 degrees.
2	C	Melanie's turn was 90 degrees. 360 (her goal) minus 90 (her turn) equals 270 degrees.
3	A	360 divided by 90 is 4. The sprinkler will need to be moved 4 times in order to cover the lawn.
4	B	Subtract the measure of angle A from 430° to get the measure of angle B; 430° - 120° = 310°
5	B	Holidays and months should be capitalized. The names of seasons should not.
6 Part A	A	Titles, initials, and names of people should all be capitalized.
6 Part B	D	Street names are capitalized.
7	A	Names of cities and abbreviations for states are capitalized.
8	B	The word "semester" is not a proper noun and is not capitalized. Names of school classes that are proper adjectives (related to a proper noun such as a country) are capitalized.

Question No.	Answer	Detailed Explanation
1	B	Put the protractor with its center point on K, so that one ray points to 0°, the other ray points to 115°.
2	B	The angle is an acute angle and it is little less than 45 degrees (half of the right angle). Therefore, it cannot be 48 or 90 degrees. It is closer to 45 degrees. So, it cannot be 10 degrees. So, the reasonable answer is, the angle is 28 degrees.
3	D	Put the protractor with its center on the vertex and one ray pointing to 0°, so the other ray points to 90°.
4		Let the measure of the angle which makes $\frac{1}{6}$ of a whole turn be S. We know that one whole turn is equal to 360°. Therefore, the measure of the angle which makes $\frac{1}{6}$ of a whole turn can be calculated by multiplying $\frac{1}{6}$ by 360°. Measure of angles $S = \frac{1}{6} \times 360° = \frac{1 \times 360°}{6} = \frac{360°}{6} = 60°$. One shaded cell = 10 degrees. Therefore, we have to shade $60 \div 10 = 6$ cells.

Question No.	Answer	Detailed Explanation
5	D	The fourth choice is the only sentence that is punctuated correctly.
6	D	Use commas and quotation marks to highlight direct speech.
7	B	Commas are used before the coordinating conjunction in a compound sentence. The comma in the sentence is not needed. It is not a compound sentence because it has only one subject.
8	A	Use commas and other punctuation to highlight direct speech.

Question No.	Answer	Detailed Explanation
1	A	The measure of the angle PQR is the sum of angle 1 & angle 2, so it is 40 + 30 = 70.
2	D	The measure of angle BDC can be found by subtracting 95 degrees from 120 degrees, for 25 degrees
3	B	Measure of Angle LNM = 100 - (25 + 35) = 100 - 60 = 40
4	B	The sum of the measures of the angles ∠DBC and ∠ABD is equal to the measure of the ∠ABC. ∠ABC is a straight angle. It measures 180°. Therefore, ∠ABD + ∠DBC = 180° x° = 180° - ∠DBC = 180° - 50° = 130° The sum of the measures of the angles ∠ABE and ∠ABD is equal to the measure of the ∠EBD. ∠EBD is a straight angle. It measures 180°. Therefore, ∠ABE + ∠ABD = 180° y° = 180° - ∠ABD = 180° - 130° = 50°
5	D	*Clarify* is the correctly spelled word that best fits the sentence. *Carefully* is also spelled correctly, but it does not make sense in the sentence.
6	B	*Vehicle* is the correct spelling.
7	A	*Pollution* is the correct spelling.
8	C	Avenue is the correctly spelled word.

Question No.	Answer	Detailed Explanation
1	B	Quadrilaterals are 4 sided-polygons. The prefix "quad" means 4. A rhombus has 4 sides.
2	D	The prefix "pent" means 5.
3	B	Vertices are points where two line segments meet, or intersect. Four line segments meet at Point F.
4	A & C	A line segment is straight and has two endpoints. In the figure, $\overline{AE}$ and are $\overline{DC}$ line segments. Therefore, option (B) is wrong. A ray is straight and has one endpoint. In the figure, $\overrightarrow{AB}$ and $\overrightarrow{BC}$ are rays. Therefore, option (B) is correct. Note that ray $\overrightarrow{AB}$ means it starts at A and goes through B and extends infinitely in that direction. So, $\overrightarrow{AB}$ is not the same as $\overrightarrow{BA}$. A line is straight and extends infinitely in both the directions. In the figure, $\overleftrightarrow{DE}$ is a line. Therefore, option (C) is correct.
5	B	"Strutted" makes the most sense in the sentence. Although all of the choices are verbs that could describe how a person enters a room, "strutted" emphasizes walking with a sense of pride.
6	B	"Grueling" means extremely tiring and demanding. While the job may be described as "uncomfortable," "grueling" describes the work more emphatically, based the context of the second sentence.
7	C	"Elated" is the most precise word choice. The second sentence gives context indicating that Dante was excited about his award.
8	A	"Gigantic" makes the most sense in this sentence. While "big" could also describe the mess, it is not as expressive. "Gigantic" gives the reader an idea of how big the mess was.

Question No.	Answer	Detailed Explanation
1	C	The hands of this clock differ by 90 degrees. So, the answer is Right angle.
2	D	Obtuse angles are larger than 90 degrees; acute angles are smaller than 90 degrees.
3	D	Right angles are 90 degrees, acute angles are less than 90 degrees and obtuse angles are more than 90 degrees.
4	A,B & D	The letter L has one right angle, the letter T has two right angles, and the letter E has three right angles.
5	D	The fourth answer choice is correct. In the first choice there aren't any quotation marks to indicate speech; the second choice implies a third person is speaking; and the third choice would need an apostrophe "s" after "Jermaine" (with a lower case "m") in order to be correct.
6	B	The second answer choice is correct. It is the only choice that implies another character is speaking, and it has an exclamation point at the end to indicate excitement or shouting.
7	C	An exclamation point is the correct way to end this sentence. Dante is very excited about his award.
8	D	The fourth answer choice is correct. This is neither a question, nor an exclamatory sentence. The third answer choice is without punctuation.

Question No.	Answer	Detailed Explanation
1	A	The names given to different types of polygons (triangle, quadrilateral, pentagon, etc.) are based on how many sides or interior angles each figure has.
2	B	The prefix "quad" means 4.
3	B	The opposite sides of a rectangle must be congruent and parallel. In addition to this, each of the 4 angles of a rectangle measure 90 degrees.

4		

	true	false
An acute triangle can be an equilateral triangle	○	
An acute triangle cannot be an isosceles triangle		○
An acute triangle cannot be a scalene triangle		○
All right triangles are scalene triangles		○
An obtuse triangle can be an isosceles triangle		
An obtuse triangle can be a scalene triangle	○	

An acute triangle can be any of the three triangles: equilateral or isosceles or scalene. Examples : An acute triangle whose angles measure 60°, 60° and 60° is an equilateral triangle. An acute triangle whose angles measure 80°, 80° and 20° is an acute isosceles triangle. An acute triangle whose angles measure 75°, 65° and 40° is an acute scalene triangle.

A right triangle can be an isosceles triangle or a scalene triangle (It cannot be an equilateral triangle because each angle in an equilateral triangle measures 60°). A right triangle whose angles measure 90°, 45° and 45° is a right isosceles triangle. A right triangle whose angles measure 90°, 65° and 25° is a right scalene triangle.

An obtuse triangle can be an isosceles triangle or a scalene triangle (It cannot be an equilateral triangle because each angle in an equilateral triangle measures 60°). An obtuse triangle whose angles measure 120°, 30° and 30° is an obtuse isosceles triangle. An obtuse triangle whose angles measure 130°, 30° and 20° is an obtuse scalene triangle.

5	B	Extracted means took out. The milk is taken out of the coconut.
6	C	After losing everything in a fire, a person would be really sad and upset. Disheartened means very upset.
7	B	We know that it means comfort, because dad did it after the girl's dog died.
8	D	We know the kittens are in bed against their mother, so it means "snuggled up to."

Week 7

Question No.	Answer	Detailed Explanation
1	B	A line of symmetry is an imaginary line that separates a figure into identical parts.
2	C	For regular polygons, the number of lines of symmetry equals the number of sides the shape has. A pentagon has 5 sides, so there are 5 lines of symmetry.
3	B	A rectangle has two lines of symmetry. One is horizontal through its center, the other is vertical through its center.
4		The line of symmetry is the line that is where you can fold and have two identical halves.
5	B	"Sentiment," is a view or attitude toward a situation or event, in this case the suffering of Americans during the Great Depression. Roosevelt's view was that the biggest obstacle to progress was fear. The other answer choices do not make sense in the paragraph.
6	B	"Assuage," means "to ease." The words Roosevelt shared in his speech helped to ease people's fear. The second sentence says, "giving them hope." This provides context that assuage is a positive word and that Roosevelt made them feel better, not worse.
7	B	"Affluent" means wealthy or having a lot of money. Context clues are that the food was expensive and patrons had to dress nicely.
8	D	"Patrons" are customers. The context clue is that they had to, "dress nicely in <u>order to eat there</u>." The customers of a restaurant are the people who eat there, unlike the cooks or the waiters. "Doctors" is unrelated to the clues in the paragraph.

Question No.	Answer	Detailed Explanation
1	A	It is known that Cindy's mother baked 4 + 3 + 4 dozens of cookies plus an unknown number (n). The correct equation adds the amount baked Monday through Wednesday and adds the unknown (n).
2	B	47 divided by 9 = 5 with a remainder of 2.
3	D	There is a difference between the number of visitors to the science exhibit and the number of adult visitors. Subtract 63 from 147 to find n. The inverse equation is the correct answer: 63 + n = 147
4	18 - 6 = 12	Let the number of chocolates Tim had be N He gave 6 to his friends. Hence, the balance will be N - 6 So, the number of chocolates left with him will be 18 - 6 = 12
5	B	"Dis-" is a prefix meaning *not or opposite of*.
6	C	"Re-" is a prefix that means *again*.
7	B	"Hemi" is a prefix that means *half*, so *hemisphere* refers to half of the earth.
8	be	"Be-" is a prefix added to the word "wailed."

Question No.	Answer	Detailed Explanation
1	D	This problem requires 2 steps. There were (5) 18 count packs bought. Multiply 5 x 18 = 90. There were (10) 24 count packs bought. Multiply 10 x 24 = 240. Add the two products together to find out the sum or total amount bought. 240 + 90, which equals 330.
2	C	The question begins with the word, "about", which means to estimate. Begin by rounding off the number of cookies. 48 rounds off to 50. Multiply that estimate by the number of boxes: 50 x 18 = 900. Of the four estimate choices, 1,000 is the closest estimate. Also note 18 can be rounded to 20.
3	A	This is a subtraction problem. There are 60 female teachers, however, there are 16 more of them than male teachers. Hence, the number of male teachers will be 60 - 16.

Question 4:

	Multiplier	Number in original set	Number in second bag
48	○	○	●
8	○	●	○
6	●	○	○

He had 8 pennies in the first bag, so that is the number in the original set. It says the second bag has 6 times as many pennies as the first bag, so 6 is our multiplier. 8 x 6 = 48 pennies in the second bag.

Question No.	Answer	Detailed Explanation
5	A	The first choice is correct. Textbook glossaries contain definitions of key words in the textbook.
6	D	The fourth choice is correct. The "n." at the beginning of the entry tells the reader that the word is a noun.
7	B	The second choice is correct. The entry word in a thesaurus is followed by the part of speech and a list of synonyms. Antonyms are also frequently listed after that.
8	B	The second choice is correct. It is the only word not listed as a synonym.

Question No.	Answer	Detailed Explanation
1	A	The best option for the supplier would be to use as many large boxes as possible. The supplier would be able to ship 600 jars in 10 large boxes and 100 jars in 4 small boxes. The supplier could not use any more large boxes, because 11 large boxes would contain 660 jars. That would leave 40 more jars to be shipped. That cannot be done without sending a partially-filled box.
2	D	If Allison were to buy 10 ropes, she would have 360 feet of rope. (36 x 10 = 360) Buying one more rope would bring her total up to 396 feet. (360 + 36 = 396) She is still 4 feet short. Therefore, Allison will have to buy 12 ropes in order to get at least 400 feet of rope.
3	A	Because the problem is asking about the number of rides each girl could go on, you can focus just on Katie. Katie brought $20.00 with her to the fair. After paying the $4.00 admission fee, she has $16.00 left over. If each ride required two tickets, and the tickets are each worth 50 cents each, then each ride costs $1.00 per person. With $16.00 left over, Katie could go on 16 rides.
4	A, C & D	To find the total number of students at each school, multiply the number of classes times the number of students in each. Hillside has 126 students and Sunny-side has 105 students. Therefore A is true, B is false, and C is true. To figure out how many more students Hillside has, subtract 126 – 105 = 21 students, so D is true.
5	B	The second answer choice is correct. The metaphor compares the sky to an angry monster. They are both purple, the thunder sounds like roaring. The stormy sky is like a monster, it is fierce and threatening.
6	B	The simile describes Mom as being like a rain cloud. Rain clouds are dark and gloomy, which matches Mom's mood.
7	A	Brick walls are strong and do not allow objects to pass through them. By comparing Kevin to a brick wall, he is saying Kevin will block his opponent from scoring a goal.
8	C	The metaphor compares Sasha to a ray of sunshine. Sunshine is considered happy like Sasha because she looked at the bright side of the situation.

Question No.	Answer	Detailed Explanation
1	C	Using the inverse relationship between multiplication and division to choose the number that is a factor of 28. 28 is a multiple of 7, so 7 is a factor of 28.
2	D	Refer to the lists of the multiples of 8 and 3. The D section of the Venn diagram is for numbers that are not multiples of 8 or 3. 41, 53, and 62 are not multiples of 3 or 8.
3	A	Any whole number greater than 1 is either classified as composite or prime. Therefore, this question is asking you to find the set that contains only prime numbers. A prime number is a number that has only 2 factors - itself and 1. The first set of numbers fits this criteria. All four of the numbers in the set have only two factors.
4	13	A prime number is a number that has only 2 factors - itself and 1. From the list of numbers given, 13 is the only prime number. The correct answer is 13.
5	B	'Hit the ceiling' means to get very angry.
6	C	'Swallow your pride' means to ignore your pride and do something anyway.
7	C	'Walking on air' means really happy.
8	A	"It's raining cats and dogs" means that it is really raining a lot and hard outside.

Question No.	Answer	Detailed Explanation
1	C	Identify the relationship between the first two and last two numbers. In this case, they are increasing through addition or multiplication. Ask yourself: 24 + ___ = 36 or are all of these numbers multiples of another number. Ask the same question regarding 60 and 72. Using addition, reverse the action: 36 - 24 = ? and 72 - 60 = ? That is the missing number.
2	D	The numbers in this pattern are increasing and decreasing: 0 to 10 is an increase of 10 numbers. 10 to 8 is a decrease of 2 numbers. 8 to 18 is an increase of 10 numbers. Continue to calculate the pattern in this fashion to determine the next two numbers.
3	C	Continue to skip count by 5's from 17. List the numbers to determine which one will be a part of the pattern. So far, all of the numbers end in a 2 and a 7.

4						

1	**2**	3	4	**5**	6
2	4	**6**	8	10	**12**
6	12	18	**24**	30	36
10	**14**	18	22	26	**30**

To find the pattern, look at the differences of each pattern. In the first, they are adding by 1. In the second pattern, they are adding by 2. In the third pattern, they are adding by 6. In the last pattern, they are adding by 4. Knowing the pattern, all you have to do is add the given pattern to the previous term, or subtract the given pattern from the next term.

Question No.	Answer	Detailed Explanation
5	D	"Miniature" and "minute" are synonyms of "small." Synonyms are words that have the same meaning.
6	B	"Noteworthy" and "important" are synonyms, or words that have the same meaning.
7	A	"Radiant" and "dull" are antonyms, or words that have the opposite.
8	Glance, glimpse, look, watch	Synonyms are words which have the same meaning as the given word. Glance, glimpse, look, watch mean the same as Peek. Hence, these are the synonyms. Stare and Ogle mean the opposite which are opposites.

Question No.	Answer	Detailed Explanation
1	C	Number 3 is in the "ones" place. Number 2 is in the "tens" place. Number 9 is the "hundreds" place. The "thousands" place is next.
2	D	The 8 is in the ten thousands place, which is 8 x 10,000.
3	B	Write the 4 in the thousands place, the 6 in the hundreds place, the 0 in the tens place and the 5 in the ones place.
4	$5000	Karen has 10 times as much money. It means we have to multiply the money John has by 10; 500 x 10 = $5,000.
5	B	The word "quizzed" makes the most sense in the sentence. It means she questioned him for details about the dance.
6	B	The word "wildlife," meaning plants and animals, is the best choice. None of the other answer choices make sense.
7	C	The word "conservationist," meaning someone who works to preserve wildlife, is the best choice here. The other choices doesn't make sense in the sentence.
8	A	The word "crestfallen," meaning disappointed, is the best choice to describe Sarah's emotion. The other choices do not make sense.

Question No.	Answer	Detailed Explanation
1	C	Compare all of the digits in the numbers: 9 x 10 is not < 8 x 10.
2	B	This form requires that every digit be multiplied by the multiple of ten that corresponds to its place value and then written as such. For example, the 9 is in the hundred thousands place, which is 9 x 100,000 and written as 900,000. Place a plus sign (+) between each term in the expanded form.
3	A	There are no thousands and no ones in this number. Place a 0 in those positions.
4	2509	Notice that there is a two in the thousands place and a 5 in the hundreds. There is not a number for the 10s, so there is a 0 in the tens place, and finally there is a 9 in the ones place. Putting those numbers in, we have 2,509.
5	D	And is the conjunction used in both sentences.
6	B	Nor is the conjunction used to connect the two sentences.
7	B	As soon as is the subordinating conjunction. It introduces the sentence.
8	or	Or is the conjunction that connects the ideas.

Week 9

Question No.	Answer	Detailed Explanation
1	A	Since the digit in the ten thousands place is 5 or greater (it is a 7), round up to the next hundred thousand.
2	A	Round this number based on the digit that is in the hundred thousands place. If it is a 0-4, the digit in the millions place will remain the same. If the digit in the hundred thousands place is a 5-9, the digit in the millions place will round up to the next digit.
3	D	The digit 9 in the ones place will cause the number to round up to the next ten. When rounding to the nearest ten, the digit in the ones place always becomes a zero.

4

	Nearest 10	Nearest 100	Nearest 1,000	Nearest 10,000
4,893 rounded to 4,890	O			
15,309 rounded to 20,000				O
32,350 rounded to 32,000			O	
523 rounded to 500		O		

When rounding to the nearest 10, look at the digit in the ones place. If that digit is 5 or more, add 1 to the digit in the tens place. If the digit in the ones place is 4 or smaller, keep the digit in the tens place as it is. That is the same process for rounding to the nearest 100, 1,000, or 10,000. The only difference is you look at the digit to the right of the digit you want to round. So row 1 was rounded to the nearest 10, row 2 was rounded to the nearest 10,000, row 3 was rounded to the nearest 1,000, and row 4 was rounded to the nearest 100.

Keeping these rules in mind, we can look at the problem in another way. We have to do checking in the ascending order. i.e. from nearest to 10, next nearest to 100 and so on.

(1) 4893 is rounded to 4890. Clearly it is rounded to nearest ten.
(2) 15,309 is rounded to 20,000. Since all the digits in ones place, tens place, hundreds place are zeros (after rounding), we have to check whether 15,309 is rounded to nearest thousand or ten thousand. If it were rounded to nearest thousand, it would have been 15,000 NOT 20,000. So, 15,309 is rounded to nearest ten thousand.

Question No.	Answer	Detailed Explanation
5	D	The simple predicate is the verb. Picked is an action verb.
6	C	You is a singular subject, so hear is the correct verb for the sentence.
7	C	She is a singular subject, so is singing is the correct future tense verb to complete the sentence.
8	C	The simple predicate is the verb. In this sentence, it is cleaned.

Day 4

Question No.	Answer	Detailed Explanation
1	B	The same rules apply when adding more than two numbers: 24 37 76 13
2	A	Line numbers up. The first one is written down and the second number is written underneath. Subtract the number on the bottom from the number on the top. If the number on the top is smaller than the one on the bottom, regroup: you cannot subtract 4 from 2, so take one from the tens place. Oops! That is a zero, so take 1 from the hundreds place. That leaves a 6 in the hundreds place. Bring that 1 to the tens place and then borrow it again. Take it over to the ones place where it is needed. That leaves a 9 in the tens place and the 2 becomes a 12. Now subtract: 702 <u>314</u>
3	C	Numbers with decimal points are added just like whole numbers, except the decimal points must be in alignment directly underneath each other, including the answer: 0.55 <u>6.35</u>
4	A & C	Options A and C are correct. After you add or subtract each expression, you see options A and C equal 4,189.
5	B	Strawberry is a clue to the meaning of the word jam.
6	A	"Waste my time" is a clue to the meaning of stand.
7	D	"Hurts my back" is a clue to the word stand.
8	A	Bank is a place to manage money.

Question No.	Answer	Detailed Explanation
1	C	The order in which numbers are grouped and multiplied does not change the product.
2	B	Even without parenthesis, the order in which the numbers are multiplied will not change the product: Multiply 4 x 3. Then multiply that product x 6. 4 x 3 = 12 and 12 x 6 = 72.
3	A	This can be solved using mental math. Multiply 5 x 20 = 100. Then multiply 100 x 8 = 800.

4

5	x	**13**	=	65
23	x	14	=	**322**
10	x	34	=	340
52	x	**2**	=	104

To find the missing number in the first row, figure out 5 times what is 65. That number is 13. The second row is the answer when you multiply 23 x 14. The third and fourth row is like the first row.

Question No.	Answer	Detailed Explanation
5	B	Second person point of view is when the writer is speaking directly to the reader.
6	C	Third person point of view is when the story is being told by someone who is not a character in the story.
7	A	First person point of view is when one of the characters in the story is telling it. Pronouns such as I and me are used.
8		If I were a musician like Celia Cruz, I would play country music, because I love country music and I would like to make people happy by playing country music.

STOP! IN THE NAME OF EDUCATION: PREVENT SUMMER LEARNING LOSS WITH 7 SIMPLE STEPS

Summer Learning loss is defined as "a loss of knowledge and skills . . . most commonly due to . . . . extended breaks [during the summertime] " (from edglossary.org/learning-loss). Many teachers have certainly had the experience of taking the first month of school not only to introduce his or her rules and procedures to the class but also to get the kids back "up to speed" with thinking, remembering what they've learned . . . and in many cases, reviewing previous content. With a traditional school calendar, then, this can mean that up to 10% of the school year is spent playing catch-up.

What's a parent to do? Fortunately, there are some simple steps you can take with your child to help your son or daughter both enjoy the summer and keep those all-important skills honed and fresh:

(1) Read!

Research supports the relationship between independent reading and student achievement, so simply having your child read daily will make a positive difference. Check out the following sources to find books that your child will want to dive into: your public library, local bookstores, online stores (Amazon, Barnes and Noble, half.com, etc.), and yard sales (if the family hosting the sale has children a bit older than your own, you stand a good chance of scoring discarded books that are a perfect match for your son or daughter's reading level).

(2) Write!

Have your child write letters to out-of-town friends and family, or write postcards while on vacation. A summer journal is another way to document summer activities. For the artistic or tech-savvy child, you may choose to create a family scrapbook with captions (consider the online options at Shutterfly, Mixbook, and Smilebox). Not only will you preserve this summer's memories, but your child will also continue to practice his or her writing skills! (See Summer is Here! Ideas to Keep Your Child's Writing Skills Sharp for more writing ideas.)

(3) Do the Math!

Think of ways your child can incorporate math skills into daily activities: have a yard sale, and put your child in charge of the cash box; help younger ones organize a lemonade stand (to practice salesmanship and making change). Or simply purchase a set of inexpensive flash cards to practice basic facts while waiting in line or on a long car ride. There's even a host of free online games that will keep your child's math skills sharp.

(4) "Homeschool" Your Child

Keeping your child's skills fresh doesn't have to cost a fortune: check out some of the Lumos Learning workbooks and online resources (at lumoslearning.com/store), and your child can work through several exercises each day. Even as little as twenty minutes a day can yield positive results, and it's easy to work in a small block of time here and there. For instance, your child can work in the book during a car ride, right before bedtime, etc. Or, simply make this part of your child's morning routine. For example: wake up, eat breakfast, complete chores, and then work in the workbook for 20 minutes. With time, you can make this a natural habit.

(5) Go Back-to-School Shopping (For a Great Summer School Learning Experience)

Check out offerings from the big names (think Sylvan, Huntington, Mathnasium, and Kumon), and also consider local summer schools. Some school districts and local colleges provide learning programs: research the offerings on-line for more information regarding the available options in your area.

(6) Take a Hike . . . Go Camping!

But "camp" doesn't always involve pitching a tent in the great outdoors. Nowadays, there are camps for every interest: sports camps, art camp, music camp, science camp, writing camp . . . the possibilities are endless! With a quick Internet search, you'll be able to turn up multiple options that will appeal to your son or daughter. And even if these camps aren't "academic", the life skills and interpersonal experiences are certain to help your child succeed in the "real world". For example, working together as a cast to put on a summer theater production involves memorizing lines, cooperation, stage crew coordination, and commitment – all skills that can come in handy when it comes to fostering a good work ethic and the ability to collaborate with others.

(7) Get tutored

Many teachers offer tutoring services throughout the summer months, either for individuals or small groups of students. Even the most school-averse student tends to enjoy the personal attention of a former teacher in a setting outside of the classroom. Plus, a tutor can tailor his or her instruction to pinpoint your child's needs – so you can maximize the tutoring sessions with the skills and concepts your child needs the most help with.

Of course, you don't need to do all seven steps to ensure that your child maintains his or her skills. Just following through with one or two of these options will go a long way toward continued learning, skills maintenance, and easing the transition to school when summer draws to a close.

SUMMER READING: QUESTIONS TO ASK THAT PROMOTE COMPREHENSION

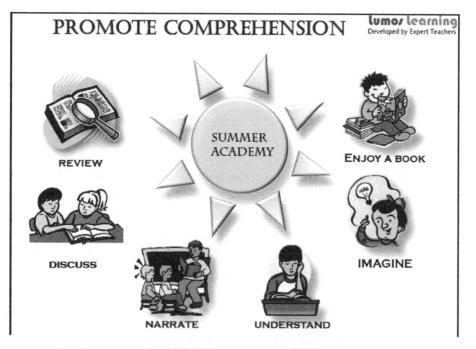

As mentioned in our "Beating Summer Academic Loss" article, students are at risk of losing academic ground during the summer months, especially with respect to their reading level, spelling, and vocabulary. One of the best ways to prevent this "brain drain" for literacy is to have your son or daughter read each day during the summer break.

Better yet, you can promote these all-important skills and participate in your child's summer reading by engaging in active dialogue with your son or daughter. Below are several questions and ideas for discussion that will promote comprehension, recall, and critical thinking skills. In addition, these questions reflect several of the Common Core standards – which underpin the curriculum, instruction and standardized testing for most school districts. Of course, the standards vary by grade level, but some of the common themes that emerge in these standards are: citing evidence, summarizing, and making inferences.

• Citing evidence

Simply put, citing evidence involves going back into the text (book, magazine, newspaper, etc.) and finding "proof" to back up an answer, opinion, or assertion. For instance, you could ask your child, "Did you enjoy this book?" and then follow up that "yes" or "no" response with a "Why?" This requires the reader to provide details and examples from the story to support his or her opinion. For this particular question, then, your child may highlight plot events he or she liked, character attributes, writing style, and even genre (type of book) as evidence. Challenge for older students: Ask your child to go back into the text and find a direct quote to support an opinion or answer.

• Summarizing

For nonfiction pieces, this may involve being able to explain the 5W's – who, what, where, when, why (and how). For literature, ask your child to summarize the story elements, including: the setting, characters, main conflict or problem, events, resolution, and theme/lesson/moral. If your child can do this with specificity and accuracy, there's a very good chance that he or she comprehended the story. Challenge for older students: Ask your child to identify more complex story elements, such as the climax, rising action, and falling action.

• Making inferences

Making an inference is commonly referred to as "reading between the lines." That is, the reader can't find the answer to a question directly in the text but instead must synthesize or analyze information to come to a conclusion. To enhance these higher-level thinking skills, ask your child to describe the main character's personality, describe how a character changed by the end of a novel, or detail how the setting influenced the story's plot. Challenge for older students: Have the reader compare and contrast two or more characters to highlight similarities and differences in personality, actions, etc.

Of course, if you read the same book that your child reads, you'll be able to come up with even more detailed questions – and also know if your child truly understood the reading based on his or her answers! But even if you don't get a chance to read what your child does, simply asking some of these questions not only helps your child's reading skills but also demonstrates an interest in your child – and his or her reading.

BEATING THE BRAIN DRAIN THROUGH LITERACY: WEBINAR RECAP WITH PRINTABLE ACTIVITY SHEET

Lumos Learning conducted webinar on "Beating the Brain Drain Through Literacy." During this webinar, we provided the students with several ideas for keeping their literacy skills sharp in the summertime.

Here's a handy chart with the ideas from the webinar, ready for you to post on your refrigerator. Let your child pick and choose the activities that appeal to him or her. Of course, reading should be nonnegotiable, but the list below provides alternatives for reluctant readers – or for those who just don't enjoy reading a traditional fiction novel. The first set of activities touch upon ideas that reinforce writing skills, while the second half addresses reading skills. There is also room on the chart to date or check off activities your child has completed.

Skill Area	Activity	Completed this activity	Notes for parents
Writing skills, spelling, and/or vocabulary	Keep a journal (things you do, places you go, people you meet)		Even though journals work on spelling skills, be sure your child understands that spelling "doesn't count". Most children like to keep their journals private, so they don't need to worry about perfect skills or that someone else is going to read/grade what they wrote.
	Start a blog		Enable privacy settings to keep viewers limited to friends and family. Check out WordPress, Squarespace, and Quillpad to begin blogging.
	Get published		The following places publish student work: The Clairmont Review, CyberKids, Creative Kids Magazine, New Moon, and The Young Writer's Magazine.
	Write letters		Have your child write or type letters, postcards, and emails to friends and family members.
	Take part in a family movie night		Watch movies that are thought-provoking to elicit interesting post-movie discussions. Other good bets are movies that are based on a book (read the book first and compare the two).
	Organize a family game night		Choose word games to work on spelling and vocabulary skills (examples: Scrabble, Boggle, and Hangman).
Reading skills: fluency, comprehension, critical thinking, decoding skills, inferencing, etc.	Pick up a good book!		Places to find/buy/borrow books include: your public library, ebooks, yard sales, book stores, your child's school library (if it's open during the summer), and borrowed books from friends and family members.
	Read materials that aren't "books"...		Ideas include: karaoke lyrics, cereal boxes, newspapers, magazines for kids, billboards, close captioning, and audio books.
	Compete! Enter a reading challenge		Scholastic Reading hosts a competition called "Reading Under the Stars" to break a world record for minutes read. Barnes and Noble gives students the opportunity to earn one free book with "Imagination's Destination" reading challenge.

Note: Reading just six books over the summer can maintain – and sometimes even increase! – your child's reading level. Not sure if the book is appropriate for your child's reading level? Use the five-finger rule: have your son/daughter read a page of a book. Each time your child encounters a word that is unfamiliar or unknown, he or she holds up a finger. If your child holds up more than five fingers on a given page, that book is probably too difficult.

However, there are some books that a child will successfully tackle if it's high-interest to him or her. Keep in mind that reading levels are a guide (as is the five-finger rule), and some children may exceed expectations…so don't hold your child back if he or she really wants to read a particular book (even if it may appear to be too challenging).

Remember, if students do some of these simple activities, they can prevent the typical four to six weeks of learning loss due to the "summer slide." And since spelling, vocabulary and reading skills are vulnerable areas, be sure to encourage your child to maintain his or her current literacy level…it will go a long way come September!

SUMMER IS HERE! KEEP YOUR CHILD'S WRITING SKILLS SHARP WITH ONLINE GAMES

Like Reading and math, free online activities exist for all subjects... and writing is no exception. Check out the following free interactive writing activities, puzzles, quizzes and games that reinforce writing skills and encourage creativity:

Primary Level (K-2nd Grade)

Story Writing Game

In this game, the child fills in the blanks of a short story. The challenge is for the storyteller to choose words that fit the kind of story that has been selected. For example, if the child chooses to tell a ghost story, then he or she must select words for each blank that would be appropriate for a scary tale. http://www.funenglishgames.com/writinggames/story.html

Opinions Quiz for Critical Thinking

Practice developing logical reasons to support a thesis with this interactive activity. Students read the stated opinion, such as, "We should have longer recess because..." The child must then select all of the possible reasons from a list that would support the given statement. The challenge lies with the fact that each statement may have more than one possible answer, and to receive credit, the student must select all correct responses. This game is best suited for older primary students. http://www.netrover.com/~kingskid/Opinion/opinion.html

Interactives: Sequence

Allow your child to practice ordering events with this interactive version of the fairy tale, Cinderella. The child looks at several pictures from the story and must drag them to the bottom of the screen to put the events in chronological order. When the player mouses over each scene from the story, a sentence describing the image appears and is read aloud to the student. Once the events are in order, the student can learn more about the plot and other story elements with the accompanying tutorials and lessons. http://www.learner.org/interactives/story/sequence.html

WEBINAR "CLIFF NOTES" FOR BEATING SUMMER ACADEMIC LOSS: AN INFORMATIVE GUIDE TO PARENTS

The "Summer Slide"

First, it's important to understand the implications of "summer slide" – otherwise known as summer learning loss. Research has shown that some students who take standardized tests in the fall could have lost up to 4-6 weeks of learning each school year (when compared with test results from the previous spring). This means that teachers end up dedicating the first month of each new school year for reviewing material before they can move onto any new content and concepts.

The three areas that suffer most from summer learning loss are in the areas of vocabulary/reading, spelling, and math. In Stop! In the Name of Education: Prevent Summer Learning Loss With 7 Simple Steps, we discussed some activities parents could use with children to prevent summer slide. Let's add to that list with even more ways to keep children engaged and learning – all summer long.

Be sure to check out:

•Your Child's School

Talk to child's teacher, and tell him or her that you'd like to work on your child's academics over the summer. Most teachers will have many suggestions for you.

In addition to the classroom teacher as a resource, talk to the front office staff and guidance counselors. Reading lists and summer programs that are organized through the school district may be available for your family, and these staff members can usually point you in the right direction.

•Your Community

A quick Google search for "free activities for kids in (insert your town's name)" will yield results of possible educational experiences and opportunities in your area. Some towns offer "dollar days", park lunches, and local arts and entertainment.

You may even wish to involve your child in the research process to find fun, affordable memberships and discounts to use at area attractions. For New Jerseyans and Coloradans, check out www.funnewjersey.com and www.colorado.com for ideas.

Of course, don't forget your local library! In addition to books, you can borrow movies and audiobooks, check out the latest issue of your favorite magazine, and get free Internet access on the library's computers. Most libraries offer a plethora of other educational choices, too – from book clubs and author visits to movie nights and crafts classes, you're sure to find something at your local branch that your child will enjoy.

• Stores

This is an extremely engaging activity – and your child won't even know he or she is learning! For grocery shopping, ask your child to write the list while you dictate. At the store, your son/daughter can locate the items and keep a cost tally to stay within a specified budget. At the checkout, you can have a contest to see whose estimate of the final bill is most accurate – and then reward the winner!

You may wish to plan a home improvement project or plant a garden: for this, your child can make the list, research the necessary materials, and then plan and execute the project after a visit to your local home improvement store. All of these activities involve those three critical areas of spelling, vocabulary/reading, and math.

• The Kitchen

This is one of the best places to try new things – by researching new foods, recipes, and discussing healthy food choices – while practicing math skills (such as measuring ingredients, doubling recipes, etc.). Your child may also enjoy reading about new cultures and ethnicities and then trying out some new menu items from those cultures.

• The Television

TV doesn't have to be mind numbing ... when used appropriately. You can watch sports with your child to review stats and make predictions; watch documentaries; or tune into the History Channel, Discovery, National Geographic, HGTV, and more. Anything that teaches, helps your child discover new interests, and promotes learning new things together is fair game.

As an extension, you may decide to research whether or not the show portrays accurate information. And for those children who really get "into" a certain topic, you can enrich their learning by taking related trips to the museum, doing Internet research, and checking out books from the library that tie into the topic of interest.

• Movies

Movies can be educational, too, if you debrief with your child afterwards. Schedule a family movie night, and then discuss how realistic the movie was, what the messages were, etc.

For book-based movies (such as Judy Moody, Harry Potter, Percy Jackson, etc.), you could read the book together first, and then view the movie version. Comparing and contrasting the two is another terrific educational way to enjoy time together and work on your child's reasoning skills.

Note: www.imdb.com and www.commonsensemedia.org are great sites for movie recommendations and movie reviews for kids and families.

• Games

Playing games promotes taking turns, reading and math skills, and strategy development. Scour yard sales for affordable board games like Scrabble, Monopoly, Uno, Battleship, and Qwirkle.

Don't forget about non-board games, like those found on the Wii, Nintendo, Xbox, and other gaming consoles. You'll still want to choose wisely and limit your child's screen time, but these electronic versions of popular (and new) games mirror the way kids think ... while focusing on reading and math skills. For more ideas, Google "education apps" for suggestions.

•Books, books, books!

Of course, nothing beats reading for maintaining skills. When you can connect your child with a book that is of interest to him or her, it can be fun for your child, build confidence, and improve fluency.

To help your child find a book that's "just right", use the five-finger rule: choose a page from a possible book and have your child read that page. Every time he or she encounters an unknown word, put up a finger. If your child exceeds five fingers (that is, five unknown words), that book is probably too challenging and he or she may wish to pass on it.

For reluctant readers, consider non-book reading options, like:magazines (such as Ranger Rick, American Girl, Discovery Kids, and Sports Illustrated for Kids), cereal boxes, billboards, current events, closed captioning, and karaoke. If you keep your eyes open, you'll find there are many natural reading opportunities that surround us every day.

Whatever you do, remember to keep it fun. Summer is a time for rest and rejuvenation, and learning doesn't always have to be scheduled. In fact, some of the most educational experiences are unplanned.

Visit lumoslearning.com/parents/summer-program for more information.

Valuable Learning Experiences: A Summer Activity Guide for Parents

Soon school will be out of session, leaving the summer free for adventure and relaxation. However, it's important to also use the summer for learning activities. Giving your son or daughter opportunities to keep learning can result in more maturity, self-growth, curiosity, and intelligence. Read on to learn some ways to make the most of this summer.

Read

Summer is the perfect time to get some extra reading accomplished. Youth can explore books about history, art, animals, and other interests, or they can read classic novels that have influenced people for decades. A lot of libraries have summer fun reading programs which give children, teens, and adults little weekly prizes for reading books. You can also offer a reward, like a $25 gift card, if your child reads a certain amount of books.

Travel

"The World is a book and those who do not travel read only a page." This quote by Saint Augustine illustrates why travel is so important for a student (and even you!). Travel opens our eyes to new cultures, experiences, and challenges. When you travel, you see commonalities and differences between cultures.

Professor Adam Galinsky of Columbia Business School, who has researched travel benefits, said in a Quartz article that travel can help a child develop compassion and empathy: "Engaging with another culture helps kids recognize that their own egocentric way of looking at the world is not the only way of being in the world."

If the student in your life constantly complains about not having the newest iPhone, how would they feel seeing a child in a third-world country with few possessions? If you child is disrespectful and self-centered, what would they learn going to Japan and seeing a culture that promotes respect and otherness instead of self-centeredness?

If you can't afford to travel to another country, start a family travel fund everyone can contribute to and in the meantime, travel somewhere new locally! Many people stay in the area they live instead of exploring. Research attractions in your state and nearby states to plan a short road trip to fun and educational places!

Visit Museums

You can always take your children to visit museums. Spending some quality time at a museum can enhance curiosity because children can learn new things, explore their interests, or see exhibits expanding upon school subjects they recently studied. Many museums have seasonal exhibits, so research special exhibits nearby. For example, "Titanic: The Artifact Exhibition" has been making its way to various museums in the United States. It contains items recovered from the Titanic as well as interactive activities and displays explaining the doomed ship's history and tragic demise. This year, the exhibit is visiting Las Vegas, Orlando, and Waco.

Work

A final learning suggestion for the summer is for students to get a job, internship, or volunteer position. Such jobs can help with exploring career options. For example, if your child is thinking of becoming a vet, they could walk dogs for neighbors, or if your child wants to start their own business, summer is the perfect time to make and sell products.

Not only will a job or volunteer work look good on college applications, but it will also teach your children valuable life lessons that can result in more maturity and responsibility. You could enhance the experience by teaching them accounting and illustrating real world problems to them, like budgeting money for savings and bills.

The above suggestions are just four of the many ways you can help learning continue for your child or children all summer long. Experience and seeing things first-hand are some of the most important ways that students can learn, so we hope you find the above suggestions helpful in designing a fun, educational, and rewarding summer that will have benefits in and out of the classroom.

Additional Information

What if I buy more than one Lumos Study Program?

Step 1

Visit the URL and login to your account.
http://www.lumoslearning.com

Step 2

Click on 'My tedBooks' under the "Account" tab.
Place the Book Access Code and submit.

Step 3

To add the new book for a registered student, choose the
○ Existing Student button and select the student and submit.

Access Lumos tedBook Online Resources

BOOK CODE

SLHG9-10ML-18526-P

Assign To ⓘ
○ Existing Student   ○ Add New student

To add the new book for a new student, choose the ○ Add New student
button and complete the student registration.

Access Lumos tedBook Online Resources

Assign To ⓘ
○ Existing Student   ● Add New student

Student Name:* Enter First Name   Enter Last Name

Student Login*

Password*

Submit

Lumos tedBooks for State Assessments Practice

Lumos tedBook for standardized test practice provides necessary grade-specific state assessment practice and skills mastery. Each tedBook includes hundreds of standards-aligned practice questions and online summative assessments that mirror actual state tests.

The workbook provides students access to thousands of valuable learning resources such as worksheets, videos, apps, books, and much more.

Lumos Learning tedBooks for State Assessment	
SBAC Math & ELA Practice Book	CA, CT, DE, HI, ID, ME, MI, MN, NV, ND, OR, WA, WI
NJSLA Math & ELA Practice Book	NJ
ACT Aspire Math & ELA Practice Book	AL, AR
IAR Math & ELA Practice Book	IL
FSA Math & ELA Practice Book	FL
PARCC Math & ELA Practice Book	DC, NM
GMAS Math & ELA Practice Book	GA
NYST Math & ELA Practice Book	NY
ILEARN Math & ELA Practice Book	IN
LEAP Math & ELA Practice Book	LA
MAP Math & ELA Practice Book	MO
MAAP Math & ELA Practice Book	MS
AZM2 Math & ELA Practice Book	AZ
MCAP Math & ELA Practice Book	MD
OST Math & ELA Practice Book	OH
MCAS Math & ELA Practice Book	MA
CMAS Math & ELA Practice Book	CO
TN Ready Math & ELA Practice Book	TN
STAAR Math & ELA Practice Book	TX
NMMSSA Math & ELA Practice Book	NM

Available

- At Leading book stores
- www.lumoslearning.com/a/lumostedbooks

Made in the USA
Las Vegas, NV
11 July 2022